Aunt Phil's Trunk Volume Five

Student Workbook

Bringing Alaska's history alive!

By
Laurel Downing Bill

Special credit and much appreciation to Nicole Cruz for her diligent efforts to create the best student workbook and teacher guide available for Alaska history studies.

Aunt Phil's Trunk LLC, Anchorage, Alaska
www.auntphilstrunk.com

International Standard Book Number 978-1-940479-36-1
Printed and bound in the United States of America.

First Printing 2017
First Printing Second Edition 2018

Photo credits on the front cover, from top left: Native shaman with totem, Alaska State Library, Case and Draper Collection, ASL-P-39-782; Eskimo boy, Alaska State Library, Skinner Foundation, ASL-P44-11-002; Prospector, Alaska State Library, Skinner Foundation, ASL-P44-03-15; Athabascan woman, Anchorage Museum of History and Art, Crary–Henderson Collection, AMHA-b62-1-571; Gold miners, Alaska State Library, Harry T.Becker Collection, ASL-P67-052; Chilkoot Pass, Alaska State Library, Eric A. Hegg Collection, ASL-P124-04; Seal hunter, Alaska State Library, George A. Parks Collection, ASL-P240-210; Women mending boat, Alaska State Library, Rev. Samuel Spriggs Collection, ASL-P320-60; Students in class, Alaska State Library, Wickersham State Historical Site, ASL-P277-015-029.

TABLE OF CONTENTS

TABLE OF CONTENTS

Welcome to *Aunt Phil's Trunk Volume Five* Workbook for Students!

Read the chapters associated with each Unit. Then complete the lessons for that Unit to get a better understanding of Alaska's people and the events that helped shape Alaska's future.

I hope you enjoy your journey into Alaska's past from the years 1960 to 1984.

Laurel Downing Bill, author

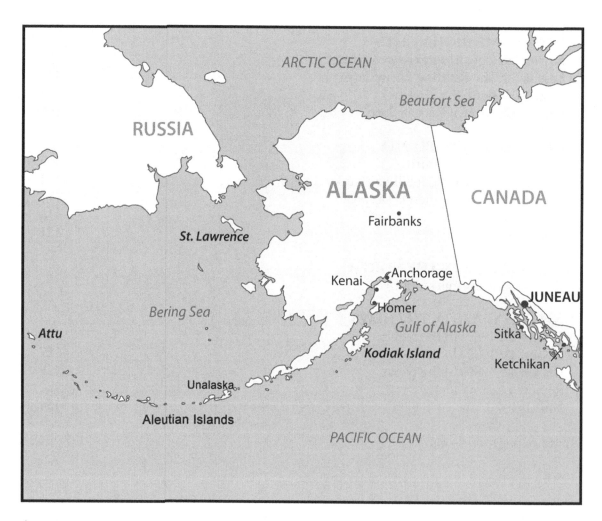

Instructions for using the Aunt Phil's Trunk
Alaska History Curriculum

The *Aunt Phil's Trunk* Alaska History Curriculum is designed to be used in grades 4-8. High school students can use this curriculum, also, by taking advantage of the essay and enrichment activities throughout the book. The next few pages give further instruction on how to use this curriculum with middle school students, high school students and in classroom settings.

This curriculum can be taught in multiple grade levels by having your older students complete all reading, study guide work and enrichment activities independently. Students of all grade levels can participate in daily oral review by playing games like Jeopardy or Around the World.

This curriculum was developed so that students not only learn about Alaska's past, but they will have fun in the process. After every few lessons, they can test their knowledge through word scramble, word search and crossword puzzles.

Notes for parents with younger students:

Enrichment Activities occasionally direct your child to watch educational videos on YouTube.com or link to other Websites to learn more about the topic that they are reading about in the lesson. You may want to supervise younger children while they are using the Internet to be sure that they do not click on any inappropriate content. This also provides a good opportunity to discuss Internet safety with your child/children.

Chapters on historical murder cases:

Chapters 36-39 contain details about historical murder cases that may be too graphic for some students/classrooms. Teachers can elect to assign these chapters for extra reading.

Please note: There are no workbook lessons for these chapters.

How to use this workbook at home

Aunt Phil's Trunk Alaska History Curriculum is designed to be used in grades 4-8. High school students can use this curriculum, also, by taking advantage of the essay and enrichment activities throughout the book. The next page gives further instruction on how to use this curriculum with high school students.

This curriculum can be taught in multiple grade levels by having your older students complete all reading, study guide work and enrichment activities independently. Students of all grade levels can participate in daily oral review by playing games like Jeopardy or Around the World.

For Middle School Students:

1. **Facts to Know:** Read this section in the study guide with your student(s) before reading the chapter to get familiar with new terms that they will encounter in the reading.

2. **Read the chapter:** Read one chapter aloud to your student(s) or have them read it aloud to you. Older students may want to read independently.

3. **Comprehension Questions:** Younger students may answer the comprehension questions orally or write down their answers in the study guide. Use these questions to test your student(s) comprehension of the chapter. Older students should answer all questions in written form.

4. **Discussion Questions:** Have your student(s) answer these questions in a few sentences orally. Come up with follow-up questions to test your student(s) understanding of the material. Older students may answer discussion questions in written essay form.

5. **Map Work:** Some chapters will contain a map activity for your student(s) to learn more about the geography of the region that they are learning about.

6. **Enrichment and Online References:** (Optional) Assign enrichment activities as you see fit. Many of the online references are from the Alaska Humanities Forum website (http://www.akhistorycourse.org). We highly recommend this website for additional information, project ideas, etc.

7. **Unit Review:** At the end of a unit, your student will complete Unit Review questions and word puzzles in the study guide. Students should review all the chapters in the unit before completing the review. Parents may want to assist younger students with the word puzzles.

8. **Unit Test:** (Optional) There is an optional test that you can administer to your student(s) after they have completed all the unit work.

How to use this workbook for high school

1. **Facts to Know:** Your student(s) should read this section in the study guide before reading the chapter to get familiar with new terms that they will encounter.

2. **Read the chapter:** Your student(s) can read aloud or independently.

3. **Comprehension Questions:** Use these questions to test your student(s) comprehension of the chapter. Have your high schoolers write out their answers in complete sentences.

4. **Discussion Questions:** Have your student(s) answer these questions in a few sentences orally or write out their answer in essay form.

5. **Map Work:** Some chapters will contain a map activity for your student(s) to learn more about the geography of the region that they are learning about.

6. **Enrichment and Online References:** Once your high schooler has completed all the reading and study guide material for the chapter, assign additional reading from the enrichment material using the online links or book lists. Encourage your student(s) to explore topics of interest to them.

Many of the online references are from the Alaska Humanities Forum website. We highly recommend this website for additional information, project ideas, etc.

7. **Unit Review:** At the end of a unit, your student will complete Unit Review questions and word puzzles in their study guide. Students should review all the chapters in the unit before completing the review.

8. **Unit Test:** (Optional) There is an optional test that you can administer to your student(s) after they have completed all the unit work.

9. **Oral Presentation:** (Optional) Assign a 5-minute oral presentation on any topic in the reading. Encourage your student(s) to utilize the additional books and online resources to supplement the information in the textbook. Set aside a classroom day for your student(s) to share their presentations.

10. **Historical Inquiry Project:** Your student(s) will choose a topic from the reading to learn more about and explore that topic through library visits, museum trips, visiting historical sites, etc.

Visit https://www.nhd.org/how-enter-contest for detailed information on how to put together a historical inquiry project. You may even want to have your students enter the national contest.

How to use this workbook in the classroom

Aunt Phil's Trunk Alaska History Curriculum was created for homeschooling families, but it also can work well in a co-op or classroom setting. Here are some suggestions on how to use this curriculum in a classroom setting. Use what works best for your classroom.

1. **Facts to Know:** The teacher introduces students to the Facts to Know to familiarize the students with terms that they will encounter in the chapter.

2. **Read the chapter:** The teacher can read the chapter aloud while the students follow along in the book. Students also may take turns reading aloud.

3. **Comprehension Questions:** The teacher uses these questions to test the students' comprehension of the chapter. Students should write out the answers in their study guide and the teacher can review the answers with the students in class.

4. **Discussion Questions:** The teacher chooses a few students to answer these questions orally during class. Alternatively, teachers can assign these questions to be completed in essay form individually and answers can be shared during class.

5. **Map Work:** Some chapters will contain a map activity for your students to learn more about the geography of the region that they are learning about. Have your students complete the activity independently.

6. **Enrichment and Online References:** Assign enrichment activities as you see fit.

7. **Daily Review:** Students should review the material for the current unit daily. You can do this by asking review questions orally. Playing review games like Jeopardy or Around the World is a fun way to get your students excited about the material.

8. **Unit Review:** At the end of a unit, your student will complete Unit Review questions and word puzzles in the study guide. Have students review all the unit chapters before completing.

9. **Unit Test:** (Optional) There is an optional test that you can administer to your students after they have completed all the unit work.

10. **Oral Presentation:** (Optional) Assign a 5-minute oral presentation on any topic in the reading. Encourage your students to utilize the additional books and online resources to supplement the information in the textbook. Set aside a classroom day for students to share their presentations.

11. **Historical Inquiry Project:** Your student(s) will choose a topic from the reading to learn more about and explore that topic through library visits, museum trips, visiting historical sites, etc.

Visit https://www.nhd.org/how-enter-contest for detailed information on how to put together a historical inquiry project. You may even want to have your students enter the national contest.

How to grade the assignments

Our rubric grids are designed to make it easy for you to grade your students' essays, oral presentations and enrichment activities. Encourage your students to look at the rubric grid before completing an assignment as a reminder of what an exemplary assignment should include.

You can mark grades for review questions, essay tests and extra credit assignments on the last page of each unit in the student workbook. Use these pages as a tool to help your students track their progress and improve their assignment grades.

Unit Review Questions

Students are given one point for each correct review and fill-in-the-blank question. Mark these points on the last page of each unit in the student workbook.

Essay Test Questions

Students will complete two or more essay questions at the end of each unit. These questions are designed to test your students' knowledge about the key topics of each unit. You can give a student up to 20 points for each essay.

Students are graded on a scale of 1-5 in four categories:

1) Understanding the topic
2) Answering all questions completely and accurately
3) Neatness and organization
4) Grammar, spelling and punctuation

Use the essay rubric grid on page 11 as a guide to give up to 5 points in each category for every essay. Mark these points for each essay on the last page of each Unit Review in the student workbook.

Word Puzzles

Word puzzles that appear at the end of the Unit Reviews count for 5 points, or you can give partial points if the student does not fill in the puzzle completely. Mark these points under the extra category on the last page of each Unit Review in the student workbook.

Enrichment Activities

Most lessons contain an enrichment activity for further research and interaction with the information in the lesson. You can make these optional or assign every activity as part of the lesson. You can use the provided rubric on page 12 to give up to 5 points for each assignment. Mark these points under the extra category on the last page of each Unit Review in the student workbook.

Oral Presentations

You have the option of assigning oral presentations on any topic from the unit as extra credit. If you choose to assign oral presentations, you can use the provided rubric to grade your student on content and presentation skills. Discuss what presentation skills you will be grading your student on before each presentation day.

Some examples of presentation skills you can grade on include:

- Eye contact with the audience
- Proper speaking volume
- Using correct posture
- Speaking clearly

Use the oral presentation rubric grid on page 12 as a guide to give up to 10 points. Mark these points under the extra category on the last page of each Unit Review in the student workbook.

Rubric for Essay Questions

	Beginning 1	Needs Improvement 2	Acceptable 3	Accomplished 4	Exemplary 5
Demonstrates Understanding of the topic	Student's work shows incomplete understanding of the topic	Student's work shows slight understanding of the topic	Student's work shows a basic understanding of the topic	Student's work shows complete understanding of the topic	Student's work demonstrates strong insight about the topic
Answered questions completely and accurately	Student's work did not address all of the questions	Student answered all of the questions with some accuracy	Student answered all questions with close to 100% accuracy	Student answered all questions with 100% accuracy	Student goes beyond the questions to demonstrate knowledge of the topic
Essay is neat and well organized	Student's work is sloppy and unorganized	Student's work is somewhat neat and organized	Student's essay is neat and somewhat organized	Student's work is well organized and neat	Student demonstrates extra care in organizing the essay and making it neat
Essay contains good grammar and spelling	Student's work is poorly written and hard to understand	Student's work contains some grammar, spelling and punctuation mistakes, but not enough to impede understanding	Student's work contains only 1 or 2 grammar, spelling or punctuation errors	Student's work contains no grammar, spelling or punctuation errors	Student's work is extremely well-written

Rubric for Oral Presentations

	Beginning 1	Needs Improvement 2	Acceptable 3	Accomplished 4	Exemplary 5
Preparation	Student did not prepare for the presentation	Student was somewhat prepared for the presentation	Student was prepared for the presentation and addressed the topic	Student was well-prepared for the presentation and addressed important points about the topic	Student prepared an excellent presentation that exhibited creativity and originality
Presentation Skills	Student demonstrated poor presentation skills (no eye contact, low volume, appears disinterested in the topic)	Student made some effort to demonstrate presentation skills (eye contact, spoke clearly, engaged audience, etc.)	Student demonstrated acceptable presentation skills (eye contact, spoke clearly, engaged audience, etc.)	Student demonstrated good presentation skills (eye contact, spoke clearly, engaged audience, etc.)	Student demonstrated strong presentation skills (eye contact, spoke clearly, engaged audience, etc.)

Rubric for Enrichment Activities

	Beginning 1	Needs Improvement 2	Acceptable 3	Accomplished 4	Exemplary 5
	Student's work is incomplete or inaccurate	Student's work is complete and somewhat inaccurate	Student completed the assignment with accuracy	Student's work is accurate, complete, neat and well-organized	Student demonstrates exceptional creativity or originality

UNIT 1: THE BIG YEAR

LESSON 1: THE PEOPLE'S GOVERNOR

FACTS TO KNOW

William A. Egan – Alaska's first elected governor and its first governor to be born in Alaska

Valdez – Birthplace of William Egan

Statehood – The status of being a state allowing for self-government

COMPREHENSION QUESTIONS

1) How did William Egan gain the tools needed to lead Alaska as it entered statehood? Consider what you learned about his past from the chapter. _____

_____

_____

_____

_____

2) William Egan suffered from glossophobia. What is it, and how did it affect him in his career? _____

_____

_____

_____

_____

3) Why was Egan known as the "father of the constitution"? _____

_____

_____

_____

_____

_____

4) When did Alaska officially become a state? Who made it official on this date?

_____

_____

_____

5) Why was William Egan admitted to the hospital just hours after he was sworn into office as Alaska's first elected governor? Who took his place as he recovered? _____

_____

_____

_____

_____

DISCUSSION QUESTION

(Discuss this question with your teacher or write your answer in essay form below. Use additional paper if necessary.)

Why do you think it was important for Alaska to achieve statehood?

_____

_____

_____

_____

_____

_____

_____

_____

_____

_____

_____

_____

_____

_____

_____

_____

ENRICHMENT ACTIVITY

Create a timeline of the life and career of William Egan beginning from his birth in 1914 to his return to duties after his illness on April 20, 1959.

LEARN MORE

Read more about Alaska's road to statehood by visiting
http://www.akhistorycourse.org/modern-alaska/statehood

UNIT 1: THE BIG YEAR

LESSON 2: MOVE THE CAPITAL

FACTS TO KNOW

Juneau – The capital city of Alaska

Alaska Bill/Civil Code – Provided that Alaska's capital would be in Juneau in 1900

COMPREHENSION QUESTIONS

1) What were some of the reasons that petitioners wanted to move the capital from Juneau?

_____

_____

_____

_____

_____

2) Why did some want to move the capital to Big Lake? _____

_____

_____

_____

_____

_____

3) How did Juneau become Alaska's capital? _____

_____

_____

_____

_____

_____

4) What was Alaska's first legislative session in 1913 like? Where did the first legislators meet? How did the legislators travel there? _____

_____

_____

_____

_____

_____

_____

5) Name another area that was considered for Alaska's capital. What happened? _____

_____

_____

_____

_____

DISCUSSION QUESTION

(Discuss this question with your teacher or write your answer in essay form below. Use additional paper if necessary.)

What are some reasons that the issue of moving the capital died in the new state legislature?

_____

_____

_____

_____

_____

_____

_____

_____

_____

_____

_____

_____

_____

_____

_____

_____

LEARN MORE

Read more about the votes to move the capital by visiting
http://www.akhistorycourse.org/governing-alaska/capitol-move-ballot-measures

MAP ACTIVITY

Locate the following cities on the map below:

1)Juneau   2) Big Lake   3) Nome   4) Fairbanks   5) Willow

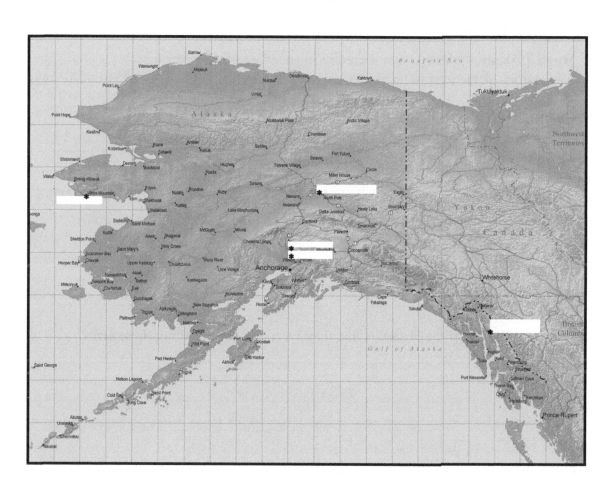

UNIT 1: THE BIG YEAR

LESSON 3: FIRST STATE LEGISLATURE

FACTS TO KNOW

Hugh J. Wade – Alaska's first secretary of state/lieutenant governor
Legislator – A member of an elected group who together have the power to make laws

COMPREHENSION QUESTIONS

1) Who led the first state legislature when it began in 1959? Why? _____

_____

_____

2) What were some of the tasks that the first Alaska lawmakers had to accomplish?

_____

_____

_____

_____

3) What were some of the obstacles that they faced in accomplishing these tasks?

_____

_____

_____

_____

4) How did the legislators fix the issue of disorganized government departments?

_____

_____

_____

_____

5) What other accomplishments did the new lawmakers achieve? _____

_____

_____

_____

_____

DISCUSSION QUESTION

(Discuss this question with your teacher or write your answer in essay form below. Use additional paper if necessary.)

What qualifications did Hugh Wade have to become Alaska's first secretary of state and acting governor as William Egan recovered from surgery?

_____
_____
_____
_____
_____
_____
_____
_____
_____
_____
_____
_____
_____
_____
_____
_____
_____

ENRICHMENT ACTIVITY

Imagine that you are the governor of a brand-new state. Write a list of all the important things that you and your team need to accomplish to set up the state. Look back at the chapter if you need help coming up with ideas. What laws need to be passed? What organizations need to be in place?

(Note to Teacher: If you are in a classroom setting, you can make this a group project. Split the students into groups, and then have each group appoint a governor to lead the discussion, a second-in-command and a secretary to take notes. Each governor will be responsible for presenting the results of the group's meeting to the class.)

LEARN MORE

Read about the legislative branch by visiting
http://www.akhistorycourse.org/governing-alaska/the-legislative-branch

UNIT 1: THE BIG YEAR

LESSON 4: FROM FOREST TO FLAGPOLE

FACTS TO KNOW

Prince of Wales Island – Island in the Southeast Alaska panhandle where the spruce tree grew that would be sent to Anchorage

Ketchikan – A small town located along the Tongass Narrows on Revillagigedo Island in Southeast Alaska

Anchorage – Largest city in Alaska, located in southcentral, where the largest flagpole stood

George H. Byer – Former Anchorage mayor and chairman of the Anchorage Parks and Recreation Commission in 1970

COMPREHENSION QUESTIONS

1) Why did many Americans refer to Alaska as "Seward's Ice Box" in the 1800s?

_____

_____

_____

_____

2) How did a spruce tree from Prince of Wales Island become a symbol of importance to Alaska in 1959? _____

_____

_____

_____

3) Why did many people think the spruce tree was a joke? _____

_____

_____

_____

4) What did George Byer say in a letter to the newspapers about the "prank"?

_____

_____

_____

_____

5) How did townspeople celebrate their new flagpole in 1959? What additional improvements were made to it? _____

_____

_____

_____

_____

_____

DISCUSSION QUESTION

(Discuss this question with your teacher or write your answer in essay form below. Use additional paper if necessary.)

What surprises were found regarding this flagpole years after it was raised?

_____

_____

_____

_____

_____

_____

_____

_____

_____

_____

_____

_____

_____

_____

_____

_____

TIME TO REVIEW

Review Chapters 1-4 of your book before moving on to the Unit Review. See how many questions you can answer without looking at your book.

UNIT 1: THE BIG YEAR

REVIEW LESSONS 1-4

Write down what you remember about:

William A. Egan _____

_____

Valdez _____

_____

Statehood _____

_____

Juneau _____

_____

Alaska Bill/Civil Code _____

_____

Hugh J. Wade _____

_____

Legislator _____

_____

Prince of Wales Island _____

_____

Ketchikan _____

_____

Anchorage _____

_____

George H. Byer _____

_____

Fill in the blanks:

1) After his father was killed in an _____, _____ was attending school and working in a local _____ by the age of 10. Since there were no restrictions on _____ at the time, the lad also learned to _____ and began _____ around his town during summers. By 14, he was _____ for the Alaska Road Commission.

2) He also learned to fly and caught the attention of _____, who arrived in his hometown of _____ in 1932.

3) Although _____ suffered from a fear of _____ _____, he was chosen chairman and presided over the _____ _____ at the University of Alaska Fairbanks from November 1955 to February 1956.

4) Many people wanted to move the capital from _____ because it is not _____ located for most Alaskans. Unlike capitals in sister states, people can't reach _____ via a road system. There are too many _____ in the way. It is accessible only by _____, providing the weather cooperates.

5) The discovery of gold deposits in the 1880s in the area that became _____ caused that town to grow in _____. A need also grew to settle boundary disputes, contracts, payments and other legal matters that necessitated travel to _____ to see a judge. Lawyers in _____ began pressuring Congress to pass a bill that would move Alaska's seat of government to their city.

6) The first Alaska State _____ met on Jan. 26, 1959, in the _____. It was led by _____ _____ because William Egan was recovering from _____ _____.

7) Alaska's _____ rolled up their sleeves and began the task of creating dozens of _____ to build the infrastructure necessary to run the nation's newest _____. And they began their business amid forecasts by doomsayers that Alaska never could survive as a state and never would be _____ viable.

8) The lawmakers accomplished many things during their first session such as: _____

_____

_____

_____

_____

_____.

9) A _____ that began life on Prince of Wales Island in the mid-1700s found its way to _____ when Alaska became America's 49th state. This Southeast sapling held no importance when Secretary of State _____ finalized the purchase of Alaska from the _____ on March 30, 1867. And most Americans at the time thought Alaska unimportant, as well, and referred to it as "_____."

10) It became the tallest _____ in the new state and displayed the new _____ at _____ City Hall in 1959. Some suggest it was a _____ originated by people in Ketchikan. According to an article in the _____ Daily News, "The theory was that it was too big a project even for 'Big _____' to complete," the article stated.

A young William "Bill" Egan became known for discussing issues and engaging in political debates at the Pinzon Bar in Valdez, seen here in the early 1930s.

Important People in the Big Year
Word Scramble Puzzle
Unscramble the words below

1. almiiwl agne

   First elected Alaska governor

2. sneret negnriug

   One-time Alaska territorial governor elected to U.S. Senate

3. dwarde elttarbt

   One of two U.S. senators that Alaskans first elected to U.S. Senate

4. parlh vrries

   Alaskans chose him as first elected Representative to U.S. House

5. wihdgt ewsoieenrh

   U.S. President who signed Alaska Statehood Bill in January 1959

6. hhgu dwae

   Alaska's first secretary of state/lieutenant governor

7. foldy inuretg

   Alaska's first commissioner of Administration

8. leicc nlotob

   Raised the first 49-star national flag at Anchorage City Hall on July 4, 1959

9. ewnarr orlyat

   First Speaker of the House in Alaska's first state legislature

10. llbeu bensett

    Alaska's first chief justice on new state Supreme Court

UNIT 1: THE BIG YEAR

UNIT TEST

Choose *two* of the following questions to answer in paragraph form. Use as much detail as possible to completely answer the question. Use extra paper in back of the book if needed.

1) Write a brief summary of notable events in the life of William Egan.

2) Why did some people want to move the capital of Alaska from Juneau? Why did others want to keep the capital in Juneau? Name at least two cities that were considered as potential capitals.

3) Who led the first state legislature? Why? What tasks did this first legislature accomplish during its first year?

4) How did a spruce tree from Prince of Wales Island become an important symbol in Alaska? Why did some consider this a prank?

_____

_____

_____

_____

_____

_____

_____

_____

_____

_____

_____

_____

_____

_____

_____

_____

_____

_____

UNIT 1: THE BIG YEAR

Review Questions	_____	(possible 11 pts.)
Fill-the-Blanks	_____	(possible 10 pts.)

Unit Test

Essay 1

Demonstrates understanding of the topic	_____	(possible 5 pts.)
Answered the questions completely and accurately	_____	(possible 5 pts.)
Composition is neat	_____	(possible 5 pts.)
Grammar and Spelling	_____	(possible 5 pts.)

Essay 2

Demonstrates understanding of the topic	_____	(possible 5 pts.)
Answered the questions completely and accurately	_____	(possible 5 pts.)
Composition is neat	_____	(possible 5 pts.)
Grammar and Spelling	_____	(possible 5 pts.)

Subtotal Points _____ (possible 61 pts.)

Extra Credit

Word Puzzle	_____	(5 pt. per completed puzzle)
Complete an Enrichment Activity	_____	(possible 5 pts.)
Oral presentation	_____	(possible 10 pts.)

Total Extra Credit _____

Total Unit Points _____

GRADE CHART

A   55-61+ points

B   49-54 points

C   43-48 points

D   37-42 points

UNIT 2: FIRST FIVE YEARS OF STATEHOOD

LESSON 5: POST ARTICLE CAUSES CONCERN

FACTS TO KNOW

Saturday Evening Post – Magazine that published an article portraying Alaska's economy in a negative light

Rebuttal – Argument or contradiction

Lester Bronson – Nome senator who thought Alaska was better off as a state

Bob DeArmond – Thought statehood for Alaska was a bad idea

COMPREHENSION QUESTIONS

1) Why did the Saturday Evening Post article titled "Alaska: Can it survive as a state?" cause concern? Summarize what the article stated. _____

_____

_____

_____

2) What were some of the rebuttals to the article? _____

_____

_____

_____

_____

3) Where did roughly 60 percent of the money flowing into Alaska in 1963 come from?

_____

_____

_____

_____

4) What were some of the signs that Alaska was becoming self-sufficient in 1963?

_____

_____

_____

_____

5) What were some of the advantages of statehood according to most Alaskans?

_____

_____

_____

_____

DISCUSSION QUESTION

(Discuss this question with your teacher or write your answer in essay form below. Use additional paper if necessary.)

Name one industry that Alaska relied upon in its early years of statehood.

_____

_____

_____

_____

_____

_____

_____

_____

_____

_____

_____

_____

_____

_____

_____

_____

ENRICHMENT ACTIVITY

Search for an article in your local newspaper or a magazine that includes a strong opinion on any topic that interests you. What rebuttals could you make to the writer of the article? Do further research on the topic if necessary. Write a short rebuttal and present it to your teacher.

LEARN MORE

Read more about Alaska's expanding economy by visiting
http://www.akhistorycourse.org/southcentral-alaska/1930-1970-the-expanding-economy

UNIT 2: FIRST FIVE YEARS OF STATEHOOD

LESSON 6: BLUE CANOES MAKE DEBUT

FACTS TO KNOW

Richard Downing – Alaska's first commissioner of public works and early proponent of the Alaska Marine Highway System

Alaska Marine Highway System – Passenger-car ferry system created after statehood

M/V Malaspina – The first ferry launched in the Alaska Marine Highway System in 1963

COMPREHENSION QUESTIONS

1) Describe the first modern-day ferry system that began in 1949. _____

_____

_____

_____

_____

_____

2) What was the "Blue Canoe"? _____

_____

_____

_____

_____

_____

3) Why did some people call the idea of the Alaska Marine Highway System "Downing's Folly"? _____

_____

_____

_____

_____

_____

_____

4) What did Public Works Commissioner Downing do to prepare for the new ferry system?

_____

_____

_____

_____

_____

5) What did Governor William Egan say about the Alaska Marine Highway System after his wife Neva, christened *M/V Malaspina*, the first ship in the new fleet? _____

_____

_____

DISCUSSION QUESTION

(Discuss this question with your teacher or write your answer in essay form below. Use additional paper if necessary.)

How did the Alaska Marine Highway improve the quality of life for many Alaskans?

_____

_____

_____

_____

_____

_____

_____

_____

_____

_____

_____

_____

_____

_____

_____

LEARN MORE

Learn more about marine transportation in Alaska by visiting
http://www.akhistorycourse.org/americas-territory/marine-transportation

MAP ACTIVITY

Using pages 74-78 of your textbook, mark the following stops along the Alaska Marine Highway System from Prince Rupert, British Columbia.

1) Ketchikan 2) Wrangell 3) Petersburg 4) Sitka 5) Juneau 6) Haines 7) Skagway

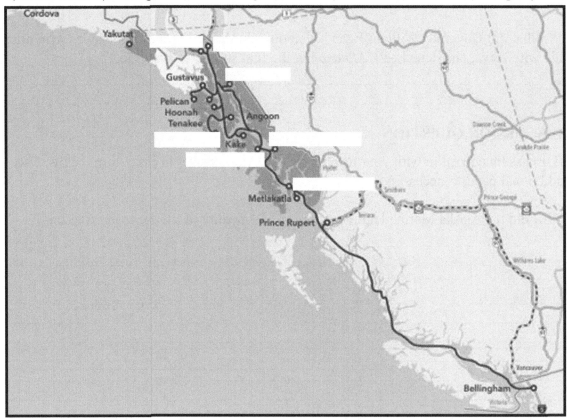

UNIT 2: FIRST FIVE YEARS OF STATEHOOD

LESSON 7: THE LOST ALASKANS

FACTS TO KNOW

Dr. Henry Waldo Coe – Founder of Morningside Hospital

Morningside Hospital – Mental health institution in Oregon where Alaskans deemed mentally ill were sent prior to the 1960s

Alaska Mental Health Enabling Act – Provided funding for Alaska's mental health care system

COMPREHENSION QUESTIONS

1) Who were the "Lost Alaskans" described in the chapter? _____

_____

_____

_____

2) What was the procedure for determining mental illness in the early 1900s? How were those who were determined to be mentally ill treated?

_____

_____

_____

_____

_____

_____

3) Why did missionaries in Anvik send James Ebana to Morningside? What happened to him?

_____

_____

_____

_____

_____

4) What deficiencies were found during government investigations into Morningside's practices? _____

_____

_____

_____

5) Why did some oppose the Alaska Mental Health Bill proposed to Congress in 1956?

_____
_____
_____
_____
_____

6) How did the Alaska Mental Health Enabling Act change the mental health care system?

_____
_____
_____
_____
_____

DISCUSSION QUESTION

(Discuss this question with your teacher or write your answer in essay form below. Use additional paper if necessary.)

Do you think that Dr. Henry Coe should have been charged with a crime? Why or why not?

_____
_____
_____
_____
_____
_____
_____
_____
_____
_____
_____
_____
_____
_____
_____
_____

TIME TO REVIEW

Review Chapters 5-7 of your book before moving on the Unit Review. See how many questions you can answer without looking at your book.

Headlines First Five Years

Word Search Puzzle

Find the words listed below

```
V  U  D  Y  I  E  K  X  S  U  G  D  I  B  C  G  Z  X  R  L
H  H  G  N  I  N  W  O  D  D  R  A  H  C  I  R  J  F  L  M
C  W  U  P  S  E  I  R  E  H  S  I  F  S  R  S  P  R  H  A
Q  P  Y  Q  J  R  Q  H  T  L  A  E  H  L  A  T  N  E  M  T
S  Q  X  I  M  B  L  U  E  C  A  N  O  E  S  Q  N  K  X  A
D  H  A  L  U  S  N  I  N  E  P  I  A  N  E  K  U  Z  F  N
M  O  R  N  I  N  G  S  I  D  E  A  M  N  T  L  U  G  N  U
O  D  R  M  S  M  A  R  I  N  E  H  I  G  H  W  A  Y  H  S
U  V  O  I  L  F  I  E  L  D  J  Q  Q  S  G  I  O  O  F  K
L  Y  H  W  F  A  F  S  T  E  G  D  U  B  J  R  T  R  D  A
T  X  T  J  V  B  F  C  H  I  L  K  A  T  R  Q  J  U  B  I
N  A  T  U  R  A  L  R  E  S  O  U  R  C  E  S  K  A  B  O
F  T  U  S  T  U  M  E  N  A  R  M  S  I  R  U  O  T  K  B
F  Q  E  N  I  L  E  P  I  P  S  A  G  L  Z  U  F  C  T  F
H  R  T  S  T  N  A  R  G  N  O  I  T  I  S  N  A  R  T  L
T  A  K  U  C  V  S  K  R  O  W  C  I  L  B  U  P  L  V  P
I  R  K  Q  U  M  N  M  K  G  Z  M  A  L  A  S  P  I  N  A
O  P  U  W  Y  M  O  N  O  C  E  P  R  R  K  Z  Z  C  G  B
A  C  P  S  Y  C  H  I  A  T  R  Y  G  A  K  L  J  T  K  R
V  D  C  D  I  F  X  W  U  N  U  D  D  L  Q  L  Y  F  E  J
```

ECONOMY	CHILKAT	TRANSITION GRANTS
FISHERIES	TOURISM	OIL FIELD
BUDGETS	PUBLIC WORKS	RICHARD DOWNING
MARINE HIGHWAY	KENAI PENINSULA	GAS PIPELINE
MALASPINA	BLUE CANOES	NATURAL RESOURCES
TAKU	MATANUSKA	TUSTUMENA
MORNINGSIDE	MENTAL HEALTH	PSYCHIATRY

The *M/V Chilkoot*, seen above loading up in Juneau in 1950, could haul 13 cars and 20 passengers between Juneau, Haines and Skagway. Once the Alaska Marine Highway System was formed in the 1960s, docks and ramps were built in Southeast towns and eventually *M/V Chilkat*, seen below, replaced the old *Chilkoot*.

UNIT 2: FIRST FIVE YEARS OF STATEHOOD

REVIEW LESSONS 5-7

Write down what you remember about:

Saturday Evening Post _____

_____

Rebuttal _____

_____

Lester Bronson _____

_____

Bob DeArmond _____

_____

Richard Downing _____

_____

Alaska Marine Highway System _____

_____

M/V Malaspina _____

_____

Dr. Henry Waldo Coe _____

_____

Morningside Hospital _____

_____

Alaska Mental Health Enabling Act _____

_____

Fill in the blanks:

1) Many were stunned when an article in The _____ titled "Alaska: Can it survive as a state?" hit national newsstands October 1963. It did not portray Alaska's _____ in a positive light.

2) The man who wrote the Post article, _____, concluded that Alaska was suffering from a "severely sick _____" that was being supported by _____. He ended the unflattering piece by saying that if the _____ did not pan out, Alaska would "remain an invalid ward of _____."

3) That Post article unleashed a barrage of _____ articles and statements from Alaskans. "A continually increasing number of new and old Alaskans could have provided Mr. _____ with a ready answer to his question," Alaska Gov. _____ wrote in a telegram to the Post. "Yes, Alaska not only will survive but will _____ as a state."

4) Gov. _____ appointed _____ as the state's first commissioner of Public Works, and _____ made creating a _____ system a priority. In January 1963, Southeasterners saw their dream of a _____ that could connect their island-bound towns with the outside world become a reality with the maiden voyage of the _____, the first ferry of the _____.

5) The author of this Alaska history series, _____, remembers some people calling the proposed ferry system "_____'s Folly" at the time – Alaska public works commissioner _____ was her father. Perhaps they said that because much of Alaska's population did not live in _____ _____ and they didn't understand the importance of connecting the communities on the _____. Some may have thought the price too _____.

6) Gov. Egan said the _____ was "perhaps the most _____ for Alaska since statehood."

7) Prior to the 1956 _____, those with mental illness were shipped off to _____ – and most families never heard from their loved ones again. They became known as "_____ _____."

8) At the time, mental illness was considered a _____ and Alaskan adults and children were _____ and sent by the federal government via dog teams, trains and ships to live at _____.

9) Alaska only had one non_____ delegate in Congress in the mid-1950s – _____. He wrote H.R. 6376, the Alaska _____ Bill. It received bipartisan support and passed unanimously in January 1956. The bill became the focus of major political controversy after opponents nicknamed it the "_____" and claimed it was part of a Communist plot to _____ Americans.

10) The _____ provided funding for Alaska's mental health care system through _____ allocated to a mental health trust. Republican Sen. Barry Goldwater helped craft the bill without the _____ provisions that had been the target of such intense opposition.

Courtesy Alaska State Library

Alaskans deemed insane/mentally ill often were made to travel through bitter cold weather to get to a port where a ship would take them south on their journey to Morningside Hospital in Portland, Oregon.

UNIT 2: FIRST FIVE YEARS OF STATEHOOD

UNIT TEST

Choose *two* of the following questions to answer in paragraph form. Use as much detail as possible to completely answer the question. Use extra paper in back of the book if needed.

1) Summarize the Saturday Evening Post article titled, "Alaska: Can it survive as a state?" What were some of the rebuttals to the article?

2) Why was the Alaska Marine Highway system important to many Southeastern Alaskans? Why did some call the idea of a ferry system "Downing's Folly"? What did Governor Egan say about the Marine Highway?

3) Describe how mental illness was treated in the early 1900s. How did the Alaska Mental Health Enabling Act change the mental healthcare system?

_____
_____
_____
_____
_____
_____
_____
_____
_____
_____
_____
_____
_____
_____
_____
_____
_____
_____
_____
_____
_____
_____
_____
_____

UNIT 2: FIRST FIVE YEARS OF STATEHOOD

Review Questions   _____ (possible 10 pts.)
Fill-the-Blanks   _____ (possible 10 pts.)

Unit Test
Essay 1
Demonstrates understanding of the topic   _____ (possible 5 pts.)
Answered the questions completely and accurately   _____ (possible 5 pts.)
Composition is neat   _____ (possible 5 pts.)
Grammar and Spelling   _____ (possible 5 pts.)

Essay 2
Demonstrates understanding of the topic   _____ (possible 5 pts.)
Answered the questions completely and accurately   _____ (possible 5 pts.)
Composition is neat   _____ (possible 5 pts.)
Grammar and Spelling   _____ (possible 5 pts.)

Subtotal Points _____ **(possible 60 pts.)**

Extra Credit
Word Puzzle   _____ (5 pt. per completed puzzle)
Complete an Enrichment Activity   _____ (possible 5 pts.)
Oral presentation   _____ (possible 10 pts.)

Total Extra Credit   _____

Total Unit Points _____

GRADE CHART

A   54-60+ points

B   48-53 points

C   42-47 points

D   36-41 points

UNIT 3: EARTHQUAKE!

LESSON 8: GOOD FRIDAY 1964

FACTS TO KNOW

Good Friday Earthquake – Historical earthquake on March 27, 1964, that hit Alaska

Richter Scale/Moment Magnitude Scale – Scales used to measure the intensity of an earthquake

Tsunamis – Destructive surges of water caused by earthquakes

Epicenter – The part of the earth's surface that is directly above the place where an earthquake starts

COMPREHENSION QUESTIONS

1) On March _____, the _____-largest earthquake in recorded history struck Alaska. It measured 8.4 on the _____ – experts later upgraded it to 9.2 on the _____ as the _____ was determined to be inaccurate at measuring earthquakes above 8.0.

2) Where was the earthquake's epicenter? Where were the effects of the earthquake felt?

_____

_____

_____

_____

3) Where did the name "tsunami" come from? _____

_____

_____

_____

_____

4) Describe some of the damage caused by the Good Friday Earthquake. _____

_____

_____

_____

_____

_____

_____

_____

5) What was the death toll from the earthquake? Why did experts state that the death toll was remarkably low? _____

_____

_____

_____

_____

6) What did Aunt Phil write in her diary after the earthquake hit? _____

_____

_____

_____

_____

DISCUSSION QUESTION

(Discuss this question with your teacher or write your answer in essay form below. Use additional paper if necessary.)

Does your family have a safety plan in the event of an earthquake? (If not, ask your parent or guardian about creating one.) What do you think should be included in your household's plan? What supplies should your family have stored in case of emergency?

_____

_____

_____

_____

_____

_____

_____

_____

_____

_____

_____

_____

_____

_____

_____

_____

_____

_____

ENRICHMENT ACTIVITY

Do you know what to do if an earthquake hits in your area? Create an earthquake safety poster that outlines what people should do in the event of an earthquake. Visit the link below for tips on earthquake safety.

http://www.weatherwizkids.com/weather-safety-earthquake.htm

LEARN MORE

Look for these books at your local library:
Earthquakes, A Primer. Bruce A. Bolt. San Francisco: W.H. Freeman and Company, 1978.

The Day Trees Bent to the Ground: Stories from the '64 Alaska Earthquake, Janet Boyland (Compiler) and Dolores Roguszka (Editor). Publication Consultants, 2005

FIELD TRIP OPPORTUNITIES

If you live in or near Anchorage, make a field trip to:

1) Earthquake Park – This historical park was dedicated to those that lost their lives in the 1964 earthquake and is the only place where you can see the devastation left by the earthquake.

Located at: 5101 Point Woronof Rd, Anchorage AK 99502
http://anchorageparkfoundation.org/directory/earthquake-park/

2) Alaska Experience Theater - You can watch a black and white movie of the 1964 earthquake and the chairs and floor actually shake you as you watch the action.
Located at: 333 W. 4th Ave Anchorage, AK 99501

http://www.alaska.org/detail/alaska-experience-theatre

UNIT 3: EARTHQUAKE!

LESSON 9: ANCHORAGE HIT HARD

FACTS TO KNOW

Genie Chance – Radio and television newscaster who interviewed dozens of Alaskans who survived the Good Friday Earthquake

Robert Atwood – Editor and publisher of *Anchorage Daily Times*

COMPREHENSION QUESTIONS

1) Summarize Robert Atwood's account of the Good Friday Earthquake to Genie Chance.

_____

_____

_____

_____

_____

2) How did Robert Atwood describe the sound of the earthquake? _____

_____

_____

_____

3) Why did Chris von Imhof jump out of a window during the earthquake? What did he compare the earthquake to? _____

_____

_____

_____

4) Describe some of the damage that Anchorage suffered from the earthquake. _____

_____

_____

_____

_____

5) Where did survivors gather after the earthquake? _____

_____

_____

_____

6) What were some of the critical issues that the city of Anchorage faced after the earthquake? _____

_____

_____

_____

_____

_____

DISCUSSION QUESTION

(Discuss this question with your teacher or write your answer in essay form below. Use additional paper if necessary.)

What award did Anchorage receive for how it recovered and rebuilt after the Good Friday Earthquake?

_____

_____

_____

_____

_____

_____

_____

_____

_____

_____

_____

_____

_____

_____

_____

_____

ENRICHMENT ACTIVITY

Watch this video to see actual footage of the damage caused by the Good Friday Earthquake: https://www.usgs.gov/media/videos/magnitude-92-1964-great-alaska-earthquake

LEARN MORE

Read more about the Good Friday Earthquake by visiting https://earthquake.usgs.gov/earthquakes/events/alaska1964/

UNIT 3: EARTHQUAKE!

LESSON 10: WILD WAVES BASH WHITTIER
LESSON 11: SEAWATER SEEPS INTO PORTAGE

Note: Read both chapters 10 and 11 before completing this lesson.

FACTS TO KNOW

Whittier – Deep-water port that lies at the western end of the Passage Canal
Portage – Area about 47 miles south of Anchorage in the Turnagain Arm

COMPREHENSION QUESTIONS

1) How did Jerry Wade describe the Good Friday Earthquake to Genie Chance? What happened to his family during the earthquake? _____

_____

_____

_____

_____

2) How did the earthquake effect the town of Whittier? _____

_____

_____

_____

_____

3) The city of Whittier, _____ in 1969, grew to around _____ people who now call it home. The town became known for _____

_____.

4) How long did the earthquake last in the Portage area? Why did it last this long?

_____

_____

_____

_____

5) What prevented the residents of the Portage area from evacuating? _____

_____

_____

_____

_____

6) How long did it take the U.S. Army to reach Portage? Why did the military have to return to Portage a few weeks later? _____

_____

_____

_____

_____

DISCUSSION QUESTION

(Discuss this question with your teacher or write your answer in essay form below. Use additional paper if necessary.)

What are some ways that we can help others during a natural disaster like an earthquake or a hurricane?

_____

_____

_____

_____

_____

_____

_____

_____

_____

_____

_____

_____

_____

_____

_____

_____

ENRICHMENT ACTIVITY

Do you have a relative who remembers the Good Friday Earthquake of 1964? If so, ask them what they remember about that day. Come up with at least three questions to ask before your interview.

LEARN MORE

Read more about tsunamis by visiting http://www.nationalgeographic.com/environment/natural-disasters/tsunamis/

UNIT 3: EARTHQUAKE!

LESSON 12: ALASKA RAILROAD DAMAGED
LESSON 13: SEWARD BURNS
LESSON 14: VALDEZ WASHED AWAY

Note: Read chapters 12, 13 and 14 before completing this lesson.

FACTS TO KNOW

Alaska Railroad – Railroad that provides rail transportation from Seward to Alaska's interior town of Fairbanks

Seward – Town located on Ressurection Bay, about 125 miles south of Anchorage via train or New Seward Highway

Valdez - Town located on Prince William Sound, about 300 miles from Anchorage via Parks and Richardson highways

COMPREHENSION QUESTIONS

Summarize how the Good Friday Earthquake effected the following places. Describe one eyewitness account for each location.

1) Alaska Railroad: _____

_____

_____

_____

_____

_____

_____

_____

_____

2) Seward: _____

_____

_____

_____

_____

_____

_____

_____

_____

_____

_____

3) Valdez: _____

_____

_____

_____

_____

_____

_____

_____

_____

4) What are some similarities you noticed between the eyewitness accounts in Chapters 12-14? _____

_____

_____

_____

_____

_____

_____

_____

_____

_____

_____

ENRICHMENT ACTIVITY

You have read several eyewitness accounts of the Good Friday Earthquake. For the remainder of Unit 3, you will be working on your own short story that takes place during the March 1964 earthquake. Take some time during this lesson to create an outline for your story. Who are your characters? In which city will your story take place? What events will you write about?

LEARN MORE

Read more about the Good Friday Earthquake by visiting https://www.ncei.noaa.gov/news/great-alaska-earthquake

Left: This map shows the 125-mile route from Anchorage to Seward along the New Seward Highway. This is basically the same route the Alaska Railroad takes, too.

Bottom: This map shows the almost 300-mile route from Anchorage to Valdez, which goes along the Parks Highway to Palmer and then changes to the Richardson Highway.

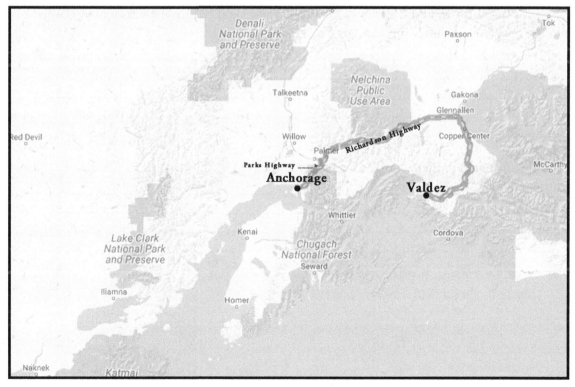

UNIT 3: EARTHQUAKE!

LESSON 15: CHENEGA DESTROYED
LESSON 16: CORDOVA AND OTHER SMALL TOWNS

Note: Read both chapters 15 and 16 before completing this lesson.

FACTS TO KNOW

Chenega – Oldest Native village on Prince William Sound; means "beneath the mountain"

Cordova – Small town located near the mouth of the Copper River

Miles Glacier Bridge – Also known as the Million Dollar Bridge; it collapsed during the 1964 earthquake

COMPREHENSION QUESTIONS

1) _____ suffered the highest percentage of loss of _____ of any community in the Good Friday Earthquake. The three giant _____ generated from the massive earthquake killed _____ villagers, more than one-third of the settlement's population.

2) How long had the Chenega people lived on their land before the earthquake? What did the survivors do after the earthquake? _____

_____

_____

_____

_____

_____

3) Did Cordova experience a lot of damage compared to other cities in Alaska? Explain your answer. _____

_____

_____

_____

_____

4) Briefly summarize how each of the following towns was affected by the 1964 earthquake:

Homer: _____

_____

_____

_____

_____

_____

_____

_____

_____

_____

Seldovia: _____

_____

_____

_____

_____

_____

_____

_____

_____

_____

Kenai-Soldotna: _____

_____

_____

_____

_____

_____

_____

_____

_____

_____

DISCUSSION QUESTION

(Discuss this question with your teacher or write your answer in essay form below. Use additional paper if necessary.)

In what ways do you think the Good Friday Earthquake changed the history of Alaska?

_____

_____

_____

_____

_____

_____

_____

_____

_____

_____

_____

ENRICHMENT ACTIVITY

Continue working on your story that takes place during the March 1964 Good Friday Earthquake. Take some time during this lesson to finish developing your characters and setting and then begin writing your story. Focus writing a strong beginning that will draw your readers into your story.

LEARN MORE

See more pictures from the Good Friday Earthquake in Alaska by visiting https://www.thealaskalife.com/blog/1964-earthquake-photo-gallery/

Courtesy Alaska State Library

Tidal waves can cause massive damage to coastal communities – this photo shows St. Michael in 1913 when a tidal wave unexectedly hit its shores.

UNIT 3: EARTHQUAKE!

LESSON 17: TIDAL WAVES OVERTAKE KODIAK
LESSON 18: VILLAGES NEAR KODIAK IN RUINS

Note: Read both chapters 17 and 18 before completing this lesson.

FACTS TO KNOW

Tidal wave – Unusually high sea wave caused by an earthquake

Kodiak – Main city on Kodiak Island that experienced strong tidal waves from the 1964 earthquake

COMPREHENSION QUESTIONS

1) How did eyewitnesses in Kodiak describe the Good Friday Earthquake? _____

_____

_____

_____

2) What was the radio report about Kodiak on the day of the earthquake? _____

_____

_____

_____

3) How much destruction did tidal waves cause to Kodiak? _____

_____

_____

_____

4) Briefly summarize what happened to the following villages near Kodiak during the earthquake:

Afognak: _____

_____

_____

_____

_____

_____

_____

_____

_____

Old Harbor: _____

_____

_____

_____

_____

_____

_____

_____

_____

Ouzinkie: _____

_____

_____

_____

_____

_____

_____

_____

_____

Kaguyak: _____

_____

_____

_____

_____

_____

_____

_____

_____

ENRICHMENT ACTIVITY

You have read several eyewitness accounts of the Good Friday Earthquake and are creating your own short story that takes place during the March 1964 earthquake. Continue developing your characters, place and plot of this story during the rest of Unit 3. Take some time during this lesson to begin writing the conclusion of your story.

LEARN MORE

Read about why Alaska has so many earthquakes by visiting https://earthquake.alaska.edu/earthquakes/about

Several tidal waves bashed Kodiak on March 27, 1964. They destroyed buildings and tossed boats into the center of town, as seen in this photograph.

MAP ACTIVITY

Locate the following places on the map below:

1) Kodiak   2) Seward   3) Valdez   4) Cordova   5) Chenega Bay   6) Whittier

7) Seldovia   8) Homer   9) Old Harbor   10) Ouzinkie   11) Anchorage

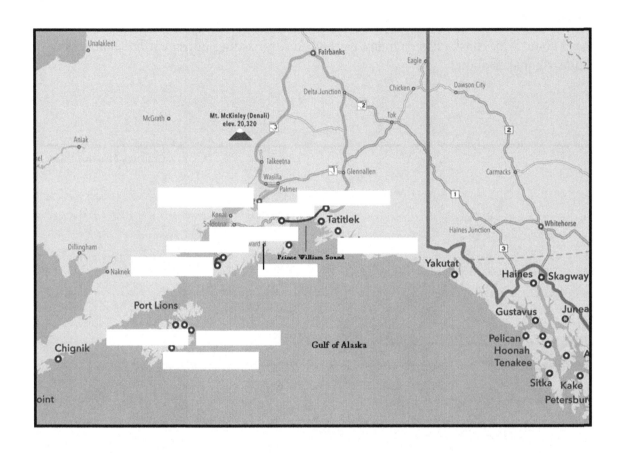

UNIT 3: EARTHQUAKE!

LESSON 19: ALASKANS LEARN THEY'RE NOT ALONE
LESSON 20: REBUILDING BETTER THAN BEFORE

Note: Read both chapters 19 and 20 before completing this lesson.

FACTS TO KNOW

The Salvation Army – A Christian organization that is one of the world's largest providers of social aid

American Red Cross – A humanitarian organization that provides emergency assistance and disaster relief

All-American City Award – Award given by the National Civic League annually to recognize 10 cities whose citizens work together to identify and tackle community-wide challenges and achieve uncommon results

Federal Disaster Relief – Federal funds used to pay for ongoing recovery projects from disasters

Government bonds – A bond is an IOU of the United States Treasury and is considered the safest security in the investment world

COMPREHENSION QUESTIONS

1) What was the overwhelming emotion that many Alaskans experienced after the Good Friday Earthquake? Who was one of the first people who shared a message with Alaskans? How did that help? _____

_____

_____

_____

_____

_____

_____

_____

2) What were some of the ways that Alaskans helped those hit hardest by the earthquake?

_____

_____

_____

_____

_____

_____

_____

3) How did Americans in the Lower 48 help the survivors of Alaska's earthquake?

_____

_____

_____

_____

_____

_____

4) Alaska's Good Friday Earthquake was ranked No. 4 on the list of major news stories for the year _____ in a poll conducted by *The Associated Press* of the nation's news editors. It was beat out of first place by the campaign and landslide election of U.S. President _____; the ouster of _____'s Nikita Khrushchev, which ranked No. 2; and the continuing _____ struggle that came in No. 3.

5) How did Alaska's earthquake alter Alaska's outlook for the future? Explain your answer. _____

_____

_____

_____

_____

_____

DISCUSSION QUESTION

(Discuss this question with your teacher or write your answer in essay form below. Use additional paper if necessary.)

Do you think that the earthquake unified Alaskans? Explain your answer.

_____

_____

_____

_____

_____

_____

_____

_____

_____

_____

_____

_____

ENRICHMENT ACTIVITY

You have read several eyewitness accounts of the Good Friday Earthquake and are creating your own short story that takes place during the March 1964 earthquake. Take some time during this lesson to write the final draft of your story. Read your story aloud to check for mistakes and/or find areas where you can improve it. Then share your story with your teacher/class.

TIME TO REVIEW

Review Chapters 8-20 of your book before moving on to the Unit Review. See how many questions you can answer without looking at your book.

Courtesy Alaska State Library

U.S. military troops immediately went into action to help earthquake victims in Anchorage. The U.S. Army Signal Corps captured this photo of the 521st Transportation Company serving hot food late into the evening following the massive quake.

Earthquake!
Crossword Puzzle

Read Across and Down clues and fill in blank boxes that match numbers on the clues

Across

3   Lack of light

5   Scattered fragments of things destroyed

7   This oldest Native village on Prince William Sound was wiped out by tidal waves

8   Break or cause to break without a complete separation of the parts

11 Great destruction

15 The point on the earth's surface vertically above the focus of an earthquake

18 Wiped out

20 Place where ships load or unload

21 These were damaged so badly that trains could not run until repaired

22 People with this type of radio transmitted messages across Alaska

25 Live through a dangerous event

26 The mainland and spit of this town dropped 2 to 6 feet

28 This city, on an island of the same name, was severely damaged by tidal waves

29 Japanese word for "port wave"

31 Day that the Great Alaska Earthquake struck in 1964

32 Save someone from danger

33 1964 Alaska earthquake measured 9.2 on this scale

37 Some people said the beginning of the 1964 earthquake sounded like this

43 Thick underlying beds of clay made the earthquake in this area last 18 minutes

45 The sliding down of a mass of earth

46 One side of Fourth Avenue in this city dropped 10 to 20 feet

47 Name of WWII pre-fabricated portable truss bridge put across creeks to connect Kenai Peninsula with road system

49 Move someone from a place of danger to a safe place

50 Exceptionally large

52 1964 Alaska earthquake measured 8.4 on this scale

54 The Elmendorf bakery made 14,000 pounds of this every day for four days

Down

1   One gets this when fuel is ignited

2   This town at the western end of Passage Canal was devastated by giant waves

4   A state of stunned confusion; dazed

6   This town on Resurrection Bay burned when oil tanks split and exploded

9   This country had the largest earthquake ever recorded at 9.5 in 1960

10 Area along which a large body of water meets the land

12 Smaller earthquakes following the main shock of a large earthquake

13 Another word for extreme fear

14 An instrument that measures and records details of earthquakes

16 A platform extending from a shore over water where boats may tie up

17 The Million Dollar Bridge near this town collapsed

19 These systems of spreading news were severely damaged

23 A sudden slip along a fault between a subducting and an overriding plate

24 A long, narrow opening of the earth

25 People had to melt this for drinking water

27 Beautiful homes in this Anchorage subdivision split and fell as a bluff broke into pieces

30 Alaska's 1964 quake released more energy than 10 million of these

34 Editor and publisher of the *Anchorage Daily Times*

35 Unable to leave because of a problem

36 Military rescue workers had to bulldoze through several of these on the New Seward Highway to get to the Portage area

Earthquake!
Crossword Puzzle

Down (Continued)

38 Physical harm to something that makes it useless
39 People stacked these in an effort to prevent flooding near Girdwood
40 A sudden event, such as an earthquake, that causes great damage or loss of life
41 This community near Portage ended up below sea level after the earth shifted and had to move

42 Another word for earthquake
44 Contaminated with harmful substances
48 Water needed to have this done in order to be safe to drink
51 Tidal waves destroyed this town situated on Prince William Sound
53 This branch of the U.S. military fed Anchorage residents for several days

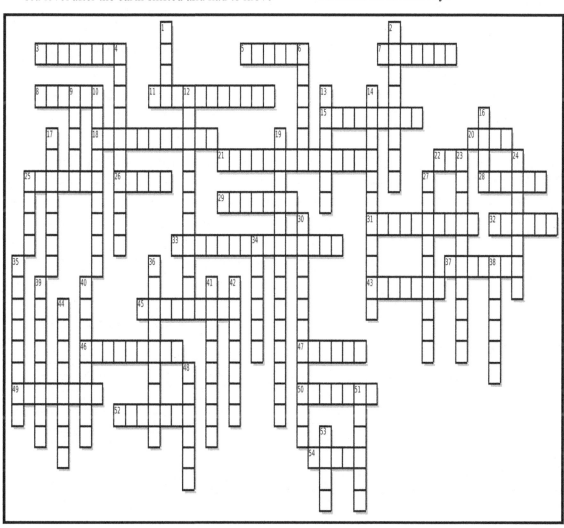

UNIT 3: EARTHQUAKE!

REVIEW LESSONS 8-20

Write down what you remember about:

Good Friday Earthquake _____

_____

Richter Scale/Moment Magnitude Scale _____

_____

Tsunamis _____

_____

Epicenter _____

_____

Genie Chance _____

_____

Robert Atwood _____

_____

Whittier _____

_____

Portage _____

_____

Alaska Railroad _____

_____

Seward _____

_____

Valdez _____

_____

Chenega _____
_____

Cordova _____
_____

Miles Glacier Bridge _____
_____

Tidal wave _____
_____

Kodiak _____
_____

The Salvation Army _____
_____

American Red Cross _____
_____

All-American City Award _____
_____

Federal Disaster Relief _____
_____

Government bonds _____
_____

Fill in the blanks:

1) The _____-largest earthquake in recorded history struck on _____. It measured 8.4 on the _____ Scale – experts later upgraded it to 9.2 on the _____ Scale as the _____ Scale was determined to be inaccurate at measuring earthquakes above 8.0.

2) The temblor's _____ was about 75 miles southeast of Anchorage, 54 miles west of Valdez and 15 miles beneath the tranquil waters of

_____.

3) _____, an adapted _____ word meaning "port wave," refers to the fact that the wave's danger and destructive power only becomes evident as it approaches the _____.

4) Radio and television newscaster _____ interviewed dozens of people across Alaska who survived the _____ Earthquake on March 27, 1964. She then compiled the interviews and published a document in 1966 titled "_____."

5) The great earthquake of March 27, 1964, destroyed the _____ at Anchorage International Airport, killing one _____ on duty that day.

6) In 1965, the National Civic League awarded _____ with the coveted _____ award – along with Seward and Valdez – for how it _____ following the Good Friday earthquake.

7) The residents of Portage had not been able to _____ due to the destruction of _____ and landslides on both sides of town. They spent a fearful night with mighty _____ hitting often, and they worried about _____ waves.

8) _____ near the docks in _____ exploded and burned during the 1964 Good Friday Earthquake. _____ from various sources created havoc on the small town, including an underwater landslide beneath the waterfront; the sloshing effect in _____ Bay; and displacement water from the earthquake fracturing the floor beneath _____ Sound.

9) Alaska Gov. _____, one of _____'s most famous residents, arrived with other state officials to survey the damage on Sunday afternoon. As their plane approached the airport, they saw tons of _____ floating on an oil-covered bay. A _____ drifted a half-mile offshore. Overturned _____ and _____ were everywhere, according to a newspaper story of the governor's visit.

10) _____, the oldest _____ on Prince William Sound, was destroyed during the earthquake. The _____ wiped out the oldest continuously inhabited _____ community in the area – a place where the _____ people had lived, fished and harvested the land for more than _____ years.

11) _____ did not suffer as much from the great quake or tsunamis as its sister cities. It did see damage to its _____, and the nearby _____ Bridge collapsed.

12) The U.S. military brought in a _____ bridge, commonly used during World War II, to connect the people of the _____ Peninsula to the rest of Alaska.

13) _____ killed 14 and caused around _____ in damage to the island town of Kodiak. They destroyed more than _____ homes, as well as _____ _____.

14) Tsunamis destroyed the village at _____. The villagers didn't think it feasible to rebuild at the same location so they rebuilt their community on Kizhuyak Bay on _____ Island and renamed it _____.

15) Old Harbor, on the southeast coast of _____, suffered subtantial damage but its residents decided to _____ in the same location.

16) Tidal waves inundated _____, on the west side of Spruce Island, about 12 miles north of the city of _____. The village existed for the _____ _____ and most villagers lost their livlihood when a big piece of the _____ was washed out to sea.

17) In those first hours after the devastating earthquake and tidal waves of Good Friday 1964, the overwhelming emotion for many Alaskans was one of _____. In most of the stricken towns, _____ and _____ dropped off the air when electricity went out. Alaskans felt _____.

18) Alaskans learned there were no _____ or _____. The earthquake not only leveled buildings, it also leveled distinctions,_____ as well as_____ and _____. Politicians forgot their differences and all Alaskans were _____ in their misfortune.

19) With well wishes from so many people all around the world, and _____ assistance from the federal _____, Alaskans did, indeed, get back to business. The motto across Alaska became, "_____."

UNIT 3: EARTHQUAKE!

UNIT TEST

Choose *three* of the following questions to answer in paragraph form. Use as much detail as possible to completely answer the question. Use extra paper in back of the book if needed.

1) What Alaska cities were most devastated by the Good Friday Earthquake? What aid was sent to the cities? How did they rebuild?

2) Summarize at least three eyewitness accounts that were covered in the unit.

3) How did the earthquake effect Alaska's economy?

4) What emotion did many Alaskan's feel after the earthquake? Why? What events helped Alaskans to unify after the earthquake?

_____

_____

_____

_____

_____

_____

_____

_____

_____

_____

_____

_____

_____

_____

_____

_____

_____

_____

UNIT 3: EARTHQUAKE!

Review Questions	_____	(possible 21 pts.)
Fill-the-Blanks	_____	(possible 19 pts.)

Unit Test

Essay 1

Demonstrates understanding of the topic	_____	(possible 5 pts.)
Answered the questions completely and accurately	_____	(possible 5 pts.)
Composition is neat	_____	(possible 5 pts.)
Grammar and Spelling	_____	(possible 5 pts.)

Essay 2

Demonstrates understanding of the topic	_____	(possible 5 pts.)
Answered the questions completely and accurately	_____	(possible 5 pts.)
Composition is neat	_____	(possible 5 pts.)
Grammar and Spelling	_____	(possible 5 pts.)

Essay 3

Demonstrates understanding of the topic	_____	(possible 5 pts.)
Answered the questions completely and accurately	_____	(possible 5 pts.)
Composition is neat	_____	(possible 5 pts.)
Grammar and Spelling	_____	(possible 5 pts.)

Subtotal Points _____ **(possible 100 pts.**

Extra Credit

Word Puzzle	_____	(5 pt. per completed puzzle)
Complete an Enrichment Activity	_____	(possible 5 pts.)
Oral presentation	_____	(possible 10 pts.)

Total Extra Credit _____

Total Unit Points _____

GRADE CHART

A   90-100+ points

B   80-89 points

C   70-79 points

D   60-69 points

UNIT 4: ALASKA LAND IN DISPUTE

LESSON 21: HOMESTEADERS HEAD NORTH

FACTS TO KNOW

59ers – Adventurers from Michigan who traveled to Alaska to seek a better life in 1959

Homestead – A piece of public land given to settlers for cultivation

President Abraham Lincoln – Sixteenth president of the United States who signed the Homestead Act in 1862

COMPREHENSION QUESTIONS

1) Who were the 59ers? Why did they travel to Alaska? How did they travel there?

_____

_____

_____

_____

_____

2) How long did it take the 59ers to reach Alaska? Did all the families make it to Alaska? Explain your answer. _____

_____

_____

_____

3) Were the 59ers welcomed by Alaskans when they arrived? Explain your answer.

_____

_____

_____

_____

4) What kind of difficulties did the 59ers face in Alaska? _____

_____

_____

_____

_____

_____

_____

5) When did homesteading end in Alaska? Why? _____

_____

_____

_____

6) Who was the last homesteader in Alaska? _____

_____

_____

DISCUSSION QUESTION

(Discuss this question with your teacher or write your answer in essay form below. Use additional paper if necessary.)

What are some of the reasons that many wanted to leave the Lower 48 and claim a homestead in Alaska?

_____

_____

_____

_____

_____

_____

_____

_____

_____

_____

_____

_____

_____

_____

_____

_____

ENRICHMENT ACTIVITY

Spend some time exploring the link below to learn more about homesteading in Alaska. Watch the video to learn about what life was like for homesteaders.
https://www.alaskacenters.gov/homestead.cfm

LEARN MORE

Read excerpts from *Alaska Native Land Claims,* a book by Robert D. Arnold, by visiting http://www.alaskool.org/projects/ancsa/landclaims/LandClaimsTOC.htm

UNIT 4: ALASKA LAND IN DISPUTE

LESSON 22: WHO OWNS THE LAND?

FACTS TO KNOW

1884 Organic Act – Provided Alaska its first civilian government and contained language that set the stage for settlement of land claims decades later

Reservations – Lands held in trust for Native people by the government

Land Claim – Petition to own a segment of land

COMPREHENSION QUESTIONS

1) Did Native Alaskans approve of Russia selling Alaska to the United States? Explain your answer. _____

_____

_____

_____

_____

2) When the U.S. Navy began governing Alaska in 1877, how did it handle disputes between the new settlers and the Chilkat Tlingits? _____

_____

_____

_____

_____

3) What protections did the 1884 Organic Act offer Native Alaskans? _____

_____

_____

_____

4) What legal step did the Tlingit and Haida people take to gain control of their land in 1935? Did it work? Explain your answer. _____

_____

_____

_____

_____

5) What was the purpose of reservations? Why did many disagree with the idea of reservations? _____

_____

_____

_____

_____

6) Why did many Native Alaskans believe that statehood would be the key to solving Native land claims issues? Was it? _____

_____

_____

_____

_____

DISCUSSION QUESTION

(Discuss this question with your teacher or write your answer in essay form below. Use additional paper if necessary.)

Why was it important for Native Alaskans to get title to land?

_____

_____

_____

_____

_____

_____

_____

_____

_____

_____

_____

_____

ENRICHMENT ACTIVITY

Learn more about Alaska Native cultures by visiting http://www.akhistorycourse.org/alaskas-cultures/alaska-native-heritage-center. Explore each link on the Webpage to read about each Native culture. Which group is most interesting to you? Why?

LEARN MORE

Learn more about the history of Native land claim issues by visiting http://www.akhistorycourse.org/governing-alaska/native-citizenship-and-land-issues

UNIT 4: ALASKA LAND IN DISPUTE

LESSON 23: ROCK, NATIVE UNITY AND LAND CLAIMS

FACTS TO KNOW

Howard Rock – Founder of *The Tundra Times* newspaper
Emil Notti – Alaska Native leader and activist who fought for Native land rights
Alaska Federation of Natives – Statewide organization formed to bring together Natives from dozens of villages and tribes to address land claim issues
Alaska Native Claims Settlement Act – Document signed by President Richard Nixon that gave 44 million acres of land and $962.5 million to Alaska Natives

COMPREHENSION QUESTIONS

1) What was "Project Chariot"? Why were Alaska Natives opposed to it? _____

_____

_____

_____

_____

_____

2) What did the Arctic Slope Native Association ask Howard Rock to start? How did this endeavor help Alaska Natives? _____

_____

_____

_____

_____

_____

3) Why did U.S. Secretary of the Interior Stewart Udall issue an injunction in 1966 to stop transfer of title from federal to state ownership? How did this help bring the issue of Native land claims to the forefront? _____

_____

_____

_____

_____

_____

4) What did Emil Notti and Willie Hensley do in May 1967 to make sure that the Native point of view about Native land claims was heard by the government? _____

_____

_____

_____

_____

_____

5) How did the oil industry play a key role in the signing of the Alaska Native Claims Settlement Act? _____

_____

_____

_____

_____

_____

6) What compromise did the Alaska Native Claims Settlement Act provide? _____

_____

_____

_____

_____

_____

DISCUSSION QUESTION

(Discuss this question with your teacher or write your answer in essay form below. Use additional paper if necessary.)

How did the Alaska Native Claims Settlement Act change the lives of Alaska Natives?

_____

_____

_____

_____

_____

_____

_____

_____

_____

_____

_____

ENRICHMENT ACTIVITY

There were many steps that happened before the Alaska Native Claims Settlement Act was signed into law by President Richard Nixon in 1971. You read about many of these in the last two chapters. Write a short summary or timeline from the Russian settlement in Alaska to the signing of the ANCSA.

LEARN MORE

Read more about the Alaska Native Claims Settlement Act by visiting http://www.akhistorycourse.org/modern-alaska/alaska-native-claims-settlement-act

Courtesy Alaska State Library

Alaska Native leaders met with then-Secretary of the Interior Walter J. Hickel, far left, to discuss the Alaska land claims dispute in Fall 1970. From left to right: Tim Wallis, President Fairbanks Native Association; Charles Edwardsen, Executive Director Arctic Slope Native Association; Eben Hopson; Emil Notti; attorney Barry Jackson (standing); State Senator William Hensley; and Alfred Ketzler. Farthest back on the right are State Senator Ray Christiansen and Frank Degnan. John Borbridge is seated in the foreground.

UNIT 4: ALASKA LAND IN DISPUTE

LESSON 24: NATIVES MUST PROVE LAND USE

FACTS TO KNOW

Land allotment – A piece of land allocated to an individual or group

Alexander Wilson – Kenaitze Indian tribe member who petitioned for his family's land

Kenaitze Tribe – Tribe of Alaska Natives who lived near the Kenai River

COMPREHENSION QUESTIONS

1) What did Alaska Natives have to prove to the government in order to receive an allotment of land under the Alaska Native Claims Settlement Act? What were some obstacles to doing this? _____

_____

_____

_____

_____

2) Summarize Alexander Wilson's account of his ancestors' use of land that he submitted to the government. _____

_____

_____

_____

_____

3) How did/do Alaska Natives view land? _____

_____

_____

_____

_____

4) According to the account given by Alexander Wilson, why did so few Indians know how to read and write their history? _____

_____

_____

_____

_____

5) Did the Wilson family ever receive their family land? Explain why the family strung glass jars around the property? _____

_____

_____

_____

_____

DISCUSSION QUESTION

(Discuss this question with your teacher or write your answer in essay form below. Use additional paper if necessary.)

What were some traditions that you learned about in this chapter? Does your family have any traditions? If so, what are they?

_____

_____

_____

_____

_____

_____

_____

_____

_____

_____

_____

_____

_____

_____

_____

_____

LEARN MORE

Read excerpts from *Alaska Native Land Claims,* written by Robert D. Arnold, by visiting http://www.alaskool.org/projects/ancsa/landclaims/LandClaimsTOC.htm

TIME TO REVIEW

Review Chapters 21-24 of your book before moving on the Unit Review. See how many questions you can answer without looking at your book.

Native Land Claims

Word Search Puzzle

Find the words listed below

```
P  T  W  A  Q  O  O  A  S  E  T  T  L  E  M  E  N  T  H  S
G  K  I  C  V  Y  Q  H  O  M  E  S  T  E  A  D  Q  B  H  E
R  T  X  G  H  G  C  H  I  L  K  A  T  P  G  C  V  A  G  D
Z  E  J  K  N  I  H  S  N  Y  F  U  F  R  B  B  I  L  K  B
R  U  S  R  H  I  C  X  H  A  B  H  S  O  A  D  O  M  E  L
O  N  C  E  E  N  L  K  R  I  P  G  F  J  A  P  S  K  N  B
C  I  O  M  R  A  L  T  A  K  A  L  T  E  M  Y  U  C  A  E
Y  N  N  I  I  V  L  B  S  L  T  Z  Y  C  M  B  B  O  I  G
M  I  G  M  T  C  A  G  N  I  O  M  Y  T  F  L  J  R  T  Z
B  L  R  Z  A  Z  N  T  O  S  S  O  X  C  R  A  F  D  Z  X
E  C  E  R  G  Q  T  U  I  O  F  C  N  H  A  R  T  R  E  C
A  H  S  G  E  K  E  N  T  O  X  S  O  A  J  T  S  A  R  L
R  I  S  D  J  Y  E  D  A  Y  N  R  A  R  A  S  P  W  X  A
C  K  T  U  I  J  K  R  R  B  R  S  X  I  N  E  V  O  T  I
O  X  N  R  M  V  L  A  E  Z  K  G  I  O  B  C  G  H  L  M
V  D  E  O  W  O  A  T  N  M  U  Q  W  T  O  N  E  F  C  S
E  D  W  R  Y  W  T  I  E  P  S  P  R  T  D  A  S  V  J  E
J  B  P  F  C  S  Q  M  G  G  M  N  A  T  I  V  E  S  Y  O
W  I  L  D  E  R  N  E  S  S  A  Y  P  I  O  N  E  E  R  S
J  T  Y  Z  W  Q  Y  S  U  K  R  U  S  S  I  A  N  S  Q  U
```

HOMESTEAD	PIONEERS	TALKEETNA
CHICKALOON	BEAR COVE	NINILCHIK
WILDERNESS	TLINGIT	RUSSIANS
CONGRESS	SETTLEMENT	CHILKAT
NATIVES	CLAIMS	HOWARD ROCK
TUNDRA TIMES	PROJECT CHARIOT	HAIDA
RESERVATIONS	ANCESTRAL	HERITAGE
KENAITZE	METLAKATLA	GENERATIONS

UNIT 4: ALASKA LAND IN DISPUTE

REVIEW LESSONS 21-24

Write down what you remember about:

59ers _____

_____

Homestead _____

_____

President Abraham Lincoln _____

_____

1884 Organic Act _____

_____

Reservations _____

_____

Land Claim _____

_____

Howard Rock _____

_____

Emil Notti _____

_____

Alaska Federation of Natives _____

_____

Alaska Native Claims Settlement Act _____

_____

Land Allotment _____

_____

Alexander Wilson _____

_____

Kenaitze Tribe _____

_____

Fill in the blanks

1) A couple of months after Alaska officially became _____, an intrepid band adventurers called the "_____," left _____ bound for Alaska. The caravan, consisting of 17 cars, six camper-trailers and a 1936 moving van named "_____" headed north on March 5, 1959.

2) In 1862, President _____ signed the _____ Act with the idea that free _____ would help develop this unpopulated area. The act took effect on Jan. 1, 1863. Special legislation extended the provisions of the act to the territory of Alaska in _____.

3) Life in Alaska proved harder than most expected, though. They encountered many of the same hardships as their _____ brethren of the 19th century, such as

_____.

4) Alaska _____, the first to settle the vast unoccupied wilderness of the Great Land thousands of years before Europeans spotted its shores, fought to hold onto _____ for generations. Most had no knowledge that _____ had claimed ownership and named it _____ when fur traders landed in the Aleutians in the _____.

5) Even though the _____ Act did not have any provisions for Alaska's Natives to gain title to their _____, it did contain language that would provide for the _____ achieved 87 years later.

6) While visiting his family in _____, _____ learned that his relatives and friends were worried about a U.S. government plan to ____ _____ and create a harbor in the Arctic for shipping minerals and other goods from northwest Alaska.

7) Environmental studies began to show that fallout from _____ after test blasts contaminated lichen, which _____ eat, and it was finding its way into humans who consumed the _____. With opposition growing ever stronger, the government backed down and shelved the idea in 1962.

8) The Arctic Slope Native Association asked _____ to start the _____. Along with journalist Tom Snapp, _____ covered issues that affected Alaska's Native people and encouraged them to have pride and respect for their _____ – and to _____ for them.

9) _____ helped set the stage for the first _____
_____ convention in October 1966.
More than 400 Alaska Natives representing 17 Native organizations met for three days in
_____ to address their aboriginal _____ rights.

10) U.S. Secretary of the Interior _____ froze Alaska's _____
_____ in 1966 until the Native _____
issue was settled. _____ joined Alaska Natives' calls
for settling the _____ issue following a major discovery of
_____ at Prudhoe Bay.

11) When Natives petitioned for _____, they had to write detailed accounts of
_____ and submit paperwork to the
Bureau of Land Management. One such account, recorded by Kenaitze Indian tribe
member _____ in 1967, described his people's
history along the _____ River.

12) Alaska Natives did not view the land as _____. As the Indian
names show, they saw every trail, creek and bend in the river as an _____
_____ and their _____ to the earth ran deep.

13) _____ family wrote the information about their
Native land _____ on a piece of paper, put it into a _____
_____ and then nailed the _____ to a tree on the land that had been used by
their _____ for generations. _____ family only received
13.3 acres of that piece.

Alaska's Native people had to prove how their ancestors had used
land that they were claiming as the Alaska Native land claims issue
made its way through Congress.

UNIT 4: ALASKA LAND IN DISPUTE

UNIT TEST

Choose *two* of the following questions to answer in paragraph form. Use as much detail as possible to completely answer the question. Use extra paper in back of the book if needed.

1) Who were the 59ers? When did they travel to Alaska and why? What challenges did they face when they got there?

2) How did the 1884 Organic Act, the Alaska Statehood Bill and the oil industry all play a part in the signing of the Alaska Native Land Claims Act in 1971?

3) Who was Howard Rock? How did he make a large impact in the Alaska Native communities?

4) Why was Native land claims such a large issue? Why did it take so long to get resolved? How did Native Alaskans view land?

_____

_____

_____

_____

_____

_____

_____

_____

_____

_____

_____

_____

_____

_____

_____

_____

_____

_____

_____

_____

_____

UNIT 4: ALASKA LAND IN DISPUTE

Review Questions   _____ (possible 13 pts.)
Fill-the-Blanks   _____ (possible 13 pts.)

Unit Test

Essay 1

Demonstrates understanding of the topic   _____ (possible 5 pts.)
Answered the questions completely and accurately   _____ (possible 5 pts.)
Composition is neat   _____ (possible 5 pts.)
Grammar and Spelling   _____ (possible 5 pts.)

Essay 2

Demonstrates understanding of the topic   _____ (possible 5 pts.)
Answered the questions completely and accurately   _____ (possible 5 pts.)
Composition is neat   _____ (possible 5 pts.)
Grammar and Spelling   _____ (possible 5 pts.)

Subtotal Points _____ (possible 66 pts.)

Extra Credit

Word Puzzle   _____ (5 pt. per completed puzzle)
Complete an Enrichment Activity   _____ (possible 5 pts.)
Oral presentation   _____ (possible 10 pts.)

Total Extra Credit   _____

Total Unit Points _____

GRADE CHART

A   60-66+ points

B   53-59 points

C   46-52 points

D   39-45 points

UNIT 5: PRUDHOE BAY OIL

LESSON 25: BLACK GOLD FOUND ON NORTH SLOPE

FACTS TO KNOW

Prudhoe Bay – Remote area of northern Alaska, called the North Slope, where an immense oil field was discovered in 1967

ARCO – Atlantic Refining and Richfield Oil Company merged to make Atlantic Richfield Oil Company, which made a huge discovery in the North Slope in 1967

John C. "Tennessee" Miller – First to drive vehicles from Fairbanks to the North Slope to prove that a road to the oil fields was possible

COMPREHENSION QUESTIONS

1) How did news of the first tanker leaving the Kenai Peninsula filled with thousands of barrels of oil have a similar effect as news of the *SS Portland* leaving St. Michael with a ton of Klondike gold in 1897? _____

_____

_____

_____

2) Why did the government limit oil drilling after 30 years of exploration at North Slope reserves? _____

_____

_____

_____

3) In what other ways did the government limit oil drilling? _____

_____

_____

_____

_____

4) What were some obstacles to exploring for oil in Alaska? _____

_____

_____

_____

_____

5) What major discovery did ARCO and Humble Oil make in December 1967? _____

_____

_____

6) Why did oil company executives from all over the world meet in Anchorage in 1969?

_____

_____

_____

_____

DISCUSSION QUESTION

(Discuss this question with your teacher or write your answer in essay form below. Use additional paper if necessary.)

Why did oil companies need to keep their oil discoveries secret?

_____

_____

_____

_____

_____

_____

_____

_____

_____

_____

_____

_____

_____

_____

_____

_____

ENRICHMENT ACTIVITY

Visit http://www.akhistorycourse.org/comic/AK_Economy_pp1-55.pdf to read an online comic book about the discovery of oil in Alaska and other adventures in Alaska's economy. Be prepared to make your own comic book in the next lesson.

LEARN MORE

Learn more about oil discovery and development in Alaska by visiting http://www.akhistorycourse.org/modern-alaska/oil-discovery-and-development-in-alaska

UNIT 5: PRUDHOE BAY OIL

LESSON 26: DEADHORSE RISES IN THE ARCTIC

FACTS TO KNOW

H.C. "Harry" Jamison – Richfield Oil's exploration supervisor for Alaska

Deadhorse – Land base on the North Slope built to house personnel and provide support for drilling operations

Prudhoe Unit – Merger of 16 oil companies that managed operations on the North Slope

COMPREHENSION QUESTIONS

1) According to oil executive Harry Jamison, what were the oil companies scrambling to do after the oil boom began? _____

_____

_____

_____

2) How did oil companies meet some of these needs? _____

_____

_____

_____

_____

3) What other problem did the oil prospectors face during this time? How did they solve this problem? _____

_____

_____

_____

_____

4) Why wasn't the pipeline built immediately after the signing of the Alaska Native Land Claims Act? How did the building of the pipeline help Alaska's economy?

_____

_____

_____

_____

_____

_____

DISCUSSION QUESTION

(Discuss this question with your teacher or write your answer in essay form below. Use additional paper if necessary.)

How did the discovery of oil change the history of Alaska – both positively and negatively?

_____

_____

_____

_____

_____

_____

_____

_____

_____

_____

_____

_____

_____

_____

_____

_____

_____

ENRICHMENT ACTIVITY

Create your own comic book or short story surrounding an adventure in Alaska's economy. Include some of the history that you are learning about in this unit. You will have the rest of this unit to complete your story.

LEARN MORE

Read more about the importance of oil to Alaska's economy by visiting http://www.akhistorycourse.org/modern-alaska/alaska-yesterday-today-and-tomorrow/alaska-economy-and-resource-development

UNIT 5: PRUDHOE BAY OIL

LESSON 27: PLANS FOR A PIPELINE PROGRESS

FACTS TO KNOW

Trans-Alaska Pipeline System – Joint venture between six major oil companies
Environmentalists – Activists who focus on protecting the earth and natural resources

COMPREHENSION QUESTIONS

1) What were some of the ways that oil companies considered transporting oil from the North Slope to market? _____

_____

_____

_____

_____

_____

2) Which two ideas proved to be the most popular? Which one was chosen and why?

_____

_____

_____

_____

_____

3) Why did Native villages file suit to halt construction of the pipeline? _____

_____

_____

_____

_____

_____

4) Why did environmental conservation groups file suit to halt the construction of the pipeline? _____

_____

_____

_____

_____

5) Why was there pressure for a domestic source of oil in 1973? _____

_____

_____

_____

_____

6) When was construction of the pipeline finally authorized? When did construction for the pipeline begin? _____

_____

_____

_____

DISCUSSION QUESTION

(Discuss this question with your teacher or write your answer in essay form below. Use additional paper if necessary.)

How did the discovery of oil change Alaska's society?

_____

_____

_____

_____

_____

_____

_____

_____

_____

_____

_____

_____

_____

ENRICHMENT ACTIVITY

Continue creating your own comic book or short story surrounding an adventure in Alaska's economy. Remember to include some of the history that you are learning about in this unit. You will have the rest of this unit to complete your story.

LEARN MORE

Look for this book at your local library: *Amazing Pipeline Stories: How Building the trans-Alaska Pipeline Transformed Life on America's Last Frontier*. Dermot Cole. Epicenter Press, 1997.

UNIT 5: PRUDHOE BAY OIL

LESSON 28: PIPELINE SNAKES ACROSS ALASKA

FACTS TO KNOW

Alyeska Service Company – Managed the construction of the pipeline
Frank Moolin – Senior project manager on the pipeline known for his work ethic
ARCO Juneau – First oil tanker to take Prudhoe Bay oil to the Lower 48 on Aug. 1, 1977

COMPREHENSION QUESTIONS

1) What were some design features that were included in the pipeline plans to meet the special challenges of transporting oil through Alaska's unique environment? _____

_____

_____

_____

_____

_____

_____

2) What was life like for those working on the pipeline? _____

_____

_____

_____

_____

_____

_____

3) Describe the steps needed to lay the pipe for the trans-Alaska oil pipeline. _____

_____

_____

_____

_____

_____

_____

4) How did the building of the pipeline increase crime in Fairbanks? _____

_____

_____

_____

_____

_____

_____

5) Was work on the pipeline dangerous? Explain your answer. _____

_____

_____

_____

_____

_____

6) When was the pipeline completed? Describe the impact that it had on Alaska. _____

_____

_____

_____

_____

_____

DISCUSSION QUESTION

(Discuss this question with your teacher or write your answer in essay form below. Use additional paper if necessary.)

How do you think Alaska would be different if the discovery of oil never happened?

_____

_____

_____

_____

_____

_____

_____

_____

_____

ENRICHMENT ACTIVITY

Finish your own comic book or short story surrounding an adventure in Alaska's economy. Once completed, share it with your teacher and/or your class.

LEARN MORE

Take a video tour of the Alaska pipeline by visiting https://www.youtube.com/watch?v=_OrAmGOFOEk

TIME TO REVIEW

Review Chapters 25-28 of your book before moving on the Unit Review. See how many questions you can answer without looking at your book.

This photograph shows construction of the pipeline up and over the Chugach Mountains on its way to Valdez. The Alyeska Pipeline Service Company said they installed 80 mechanical check valves at up-hill sections along the pipeline that close automatically in the event of a pressure loss in the line upstream of the valve. These valves prevent the flow of oil in the wrong direction back down the 48-inch-diameter pipe.

UNIT 5: PRUDHOE BAY OIL

REVIEW LESSONS 25-28

Write down what you remember about:

Prudhoe Bay _____

_____

ARCO _____

_____

John C. "Tennessee" Miller _____

_____

H.C. "Harry" Jamison _____

_____

Deadhorse _____

_____

Prudhoe Unit _____

_____

Trans-Alaska Pipeline System _____

_____

Environmentalists _____

_____

Alyeska Service Company _____

_____

Frank Moolin _____

_____

ARCO Juneau _____

_____

Fill in the blanks

1) News of the first tanker, *F.S. Bryant*, leaving the _____ Peninsula filled with thousands of barrels of oil bound for the _____ may be compared to the news of the SS _____ leaving St. Michael with its ton of _____ in 1897. It had the same effect. Instead of miners looking for _____, though, it brought _____ searching for oil.

2) Geologists believed that Alaska's _____ held the greatest petroleum potential because of its _____ with tremendous thickness of _____. Drilling done on Naval Petroleum Reserve No. 4 had shown those sediments contained both _____ and _____. Exploration moved slowly due to problems with drilling and production in such a _____, _____ region. There were no _____ to the potentially oil-rich land, and passage via _____ to Point Barrow was limited to a few weeks a year due to sea ice.

3) In 1966, the federal government put a stop to Alaska choosing any more _____ from the 103 million acres granted it under the _____ Act. U.S. Interior Secretary _____ imposed a "_____" on the transfer of _____ claimed by _____ until Congress sorted out their claims.

4) Once the huge oil field was discovered in _____ in 1968, the race was on to build the infrastructure needed to develop the resource. The land base that grew on the _____ to house personnel and provide support for drilling operations, 206 miles southeast of Barrow, became known as _____.

5) The 16 _____ decided to have two companies manage the operations on the _____. The unusual agreement between all these companies, called _____, formed two areas within the huge oil field – one for _____ and one for _____.

6) Alaska Gov. Keith Miller and most Alaskans recognized the benefits for Alaska with building an all-Alaska _____ in the _____ and agreed with the proposal to build a terminal in _____.

7) Although oil companies were not given the green light to build the _____ until 1974, they laid much of the groundwork in advance. In October 1968, three _____ formed a joint venture to _____ to transport oil from _____ to market as soon as all the legal hurdles had been addressed. The new enterprise was called _____.

8) _____ wanted to limit development in Alaska's northern _____, but many Alaskans thought they had enough _____ areas in the vast state and developing the _____ could be done in an environmentally responsible way.

9) The battle over building the _____ continued until October 1973 when, in retaliation for American support of _____ in the _____ War, Arab states declared an embargo on _____ to America. That tipped the balance in favor of a new _____ of oil rather than importing so much oil from overseas.

10) The eight-member Trans-Alaska Pipeline System created the_____ to oversee construction activities for the massive project. _____ then developed the pipeline _____ in coordination with many federal and state agencies.

11) _____ altered its plans as it performed tests on everything from the _____ zones to _____ frost. After its analysis was complete, the industry decided the best route would take the pipeline through Dietrich Pass, later named _____ Pass, on to _____ Canyon and Thompson Pass to _____.

12) Every pipeline worker was guaranteed _____ per week of pay, even if they couldn't work due to _____. _____ not only paid _____ wages, it provided the best _____ and other amenities to keep its labor force happy. Those _____ wages created a boomtown atmosphere in both Fairbanks and Anchorage. This also increased _____ in these cities.

13) When completed in _____, the pipeline crossed 34 _____, around 800 smaller _____ and three _____ ranges. It also had 11 _____ stations to help move the oil along. The _____ was built at the southern end of the pipeline.

14) According to Native leader _____, the pipeline, which has delivered billions of barrels of oil, has had some spills from _____ _____. But overall, it has worked as well as most everyone could have hoped. Alaska oil has been the _____ in U.S. history, transforming Alaska from one of the _____ to one of the _____ states in the nation.

Alaska Oil Pipeline
Word Scramble
Please unscramble the words below

1. dsaordeeh — Large land base on Alaska's North Slope where workers live

2. udrphoe yba — An immense oil field was discovered here in 1967

3. anyrtb — Name of oil tanker that carried the first shipment of oil out of the Kenai Peninsula

4. mot maarllhs — Alaska's only geologist in 1964

5. rcedu oil — Alaskans call this "black gold"

6. dilirlng rgi — Name for equipment that digs down into the earth to find oil

7. feruotab esa — Large body of water at North Slope

8. eazvdl — Southern port where trans-Alaska oil pipeline ends

9. ltoadn — Name of haul road to North Slope

10. ayalesk — Service company that oversaw the Alaska pipeline construction activities

11. pigs — equipment that goes through the pipeline to clean and gather information

12. auujne — First Prudhoe Bay oil left on this tanker in 1977

UNIT 5: PRUDHOE BAY OIL

UNIT TEST

Choose *two* of the following questions to answer in paragraph form. Use as much detail as possible to completely answer the question. Use extra paper in back of the book if needed.

1) Describe the impact that the petroleum boom in Alaska had on its population, society, government and economy.

2) Name two ways the construction of the pipeline was delayed. How were these issues resolved?

3) What were some of the obstacles to drilling and transporting oil through Alaska for market?

4) What was life like for the construction workers who built the pipeline? What kind of hours did they work? Did they make good money? Was it dangerous work?

_____

_____

_____

_____

_____

_____

_____

_____

_____

_____

_____

_____

_____

_____

_____

_____

_____

_____

_____

UNIT 5: PRUDHOE BAY OIL

Review Questions	_____	(possible 11 pts.)
Fill-the-Blanks	_____	(possible 14 pts.)

Unit Test

Essay 1

Demonstrates understanding of the topic	_____	(possible 5 pts.)
Answered the questions completely and accurately	_____	(possible 5 pts.)
Composition is neat	_____	(possible 5 pts.)
Grammar and Spelling	_____	(possible 5 pts.)

Essay 2

Demonstrates understanding of the topic	_____	(possible 5 pts.)
Answered the questions completely and accurately	_____	(possible 5 pts.)
Composition is neat	_____	(possible 5 pts.)
Grammar and Spelling	_____	(possible 5 pts.)

Subtotal Points _____ **(possible 65 pts.)**

Extra Credit

Word Puzzle	_____	(5 pt. per completed puzzle)
Complete an Enrichment Activity	_____	(possible 5 pts.)
Oral presentation	_____	(possible 10 pts.)

Total Extra Credit _____

Total Unit Points _____

GRADE CHART

A   59-65+ points

B   52-58 points

C   45-51 points

D   38-44 points

UNIT 6: SOME HIGHLIGHTS

LESSON 29: ICEWORM REVIVES CORDOVA

FACTS TO KNOW

Cordova – Small town in Prince William Sound that used the idea of an iceworm to combat mid-winter doldrums and draw tourists to town

Iceworm – Tiny black worms that avoid the sun and spend their lives in glacial ice

Ohmer Waer – Hotel manager in Cordova who had the idea of creating an "iceworm"

COMPREHENSION QUESTIONS

1) Why did Dawson newspaper man E.J. White write an article about iceworms one winter during the Klondike gold rush? _____

_____

_____

_____

_____

2) Did E.J. White make up the idea of iceworms, or do iceworms really exist? Explain your answer. _____

_____

_____

_____

_____

3) What organization did Ohmer Waer, Bob Logan, Frank Smith and Harold Bonser form in 1960? _____

_____

_____

_____

4) Describe the design of the iceworm that Cordova residents created. _____

_____

_____

_____

_____

5) How do Cordovans use the iceworm to celebrate their city? _____

_____

_____

_____

_____

DISCUSSION QUESTION

(Discuss this question with your teacher or write your answer in essay form below. Use additional paper if necessary.)

What do you think the creation of the Iceworm Festival did for the residents of Cordova?

_____

_____

_____

_____

_____

_____

_____

_____

_____

_____

_____

_____

_____

_____

_____

_____

_____

ENRICHMENT ACTIVITY

Classroom Teachers: This project can be done individually or in small groups.

You have just been put in charge of your city's visitors' association. Come up with a creative festival to draw tourists to your city and teach them more about it. Write out your plans or create a poster to advertise the festival.

LEARN MORE

Read more about art, culture, and recreation in various Alaskan cities by visiting http://www.akhistorycourse.org/americas-territory/alaskas-heritage/chapter-4-19-art-literature-science-cultural-institutions-and-recreation

UNIT 6: SOME HIGHLIGHTS

LESSON 30: THE PAINTING PACHYDERM
LESSON 31: BETTY THE FIRETRUCK

Note: Read both chapters 30 and 31 before completing this lesson.

FACTS TO KNOW

Pachyderm – Thick-skinned, hoofed mammal such as an elephant

Annabelle – Elephant that arrived in Anchorage in 1966

Alaska Zoo – Anchorage zoo started by Sammye Seawell, caretaker of Annabelle

Homer – City overlooking Kachemak Bay on the Kenai Peninsula

General Mills – National company that offered a program to exchange coupons for household items

COMPREHENSION QUESTIONS

1) Explain how Annabelle become the first pachyderm in Alaska since the ice age. ____

_____

_____

_____

_____

_____

2) How did Sammye Seawell come up with the idea to start the Alaska Zoo? _____

_____

_____

_____

_____

3) What special talent allowed Annabelle to raise several hundred thousand dollars for the zoo? How did her trainers discover and develop this talent? _____

_____

_____

_____

4) What item did the residents of Homer receive for participating in General Mills coupon program? How many coupons did they need to collect for this item? _____

_____

_____

5) How did the residents of Homer know that this was possible? _____
_____
_____

6) According to _____, the "Betty" _____ story represented a time
of _____ in the community. "In times past, the _____ didn't do
for the people, the people did for themselves," he said.

DISCUSSION QUESTION

(Discuss this question with your teacher or write your answer in essay form below. Use
additional paper if necessary.)

How did children in Anchorage play a part in the opening of the Alaska Zoo?

_____
_____
_____
_____
_____
_____
_____
_____
_____
_____
_____
_____
_____
_____
_____
_____
_____
_____

ENRICHMENT ACTIVITY

Check in on the polar bears at the Alaska Zoo by going to the live bear cam at http://
alaskazoo.org/live-polar-bear-camera. Take a field trip to the Alaska Zoo in Anchorage
and check out all the animals that call the zoo home.

LEARN MORE

Learn more about the Alaska Zoo by visiting http://www.alaskazoo.org/

UNIT 6: SOME HIGHLIGHTS

LESSON 32: A GREAT RACE IS BORN

FACTS TO KNOW

Dorothy Page – Secretary of Aurora Dog Mushers Club who had the idea for an annual Iditarod Trail race

Joe Redington Sr. – Veteran dog musher who became known as the "father of the Iditarod"

Iditarod Trail – Historic trail that runs from Seward to Nome; the annual race runs from Willow to Nome

Dick Wilmarth – Gold miner who won the 1973 Iditarod Trail Race

COMPREHENSION QUESTIONS

1) How did Dorothy Page come up with the idea for the Iditarod Trail Race? Why?

_____

_____

_____

_____

_____

2) When was the inaugural (first) race? What happened to delay the race for 4 more years?

_____

_____

_____

_____

3) How did Dick Wilmarth describe the race? _____

_____

_____

_____

_____

_____

4) How has the race changed over the years? _____

_____

_____

_____

(Discuss this question with your teacher or write your answer in essay form below. Use additional paper if necessary.)

What advantages did Dick Wilmarth have over the other mushers in the race?

_____

_____

_____

_____

_____

_____

_____

_____

_____

_____

_____

_____

_____

_____

_____

LEARN MORE

Read more about Iditarod Trail Race musher George Attla by finding this book at your library: *Everything I Know About Training and Racing Sled Dogs.* George Attla. Rome, New York: Arner Publications, 1974.

MAP ACTIVITY

Locate the following important Ititarod Trail towns/stops/bodies of water along the Northern and Southern routes of the Last Great Race:

1) Iditarod   2) Koyuk   3) Grayling   4) Nikolai   5) Anchorage   6) Ruby
7) Bering Sea   8) Kaltag   9) Wasilla   10) Shaktoolik   11) Willow   12) Ophir
13) Rainy Pass 14) Nome   15) Norton Sound

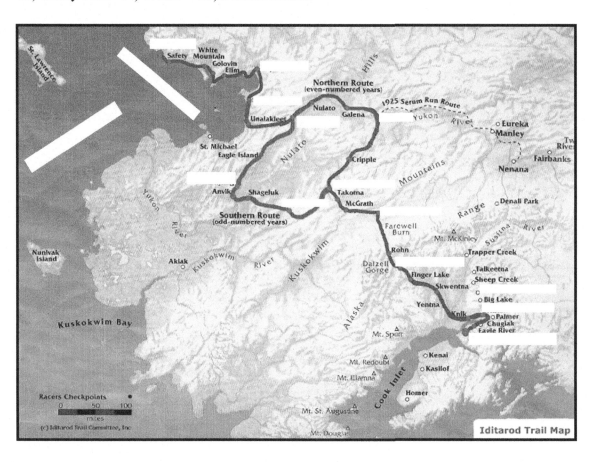

Some Highlights
Word Scramble Puzzle
Unscramble the words below

#	Scramble	Clue
1.	riecwmo	It lives in glacial ice and hides from sunlight
2.	oorcdav	Town in Prince William Sound that holds a winter festival
3.	sleicrag	Massive frozen rivers of ice
4.	nebaelanl	Name of elephant that arrived in Alaska in 1960s
5.	aaaslk ooz	An animal facility in Anchorage changed its name to this in June 1980
6.	pahymercd	An elephant is this type of mammal
7.	smemay slaewle	She was instrumental in getting a home for animals started Anchorage in the 1960s
8.	ohmer	Town in Kachemak Bay that needed an emergency vehicle in the 1960s
9.	tybet	What people named the emergency vehicle that they obtained in a unique way
10.	coonspu	Townspeople saved millions of these in order to get an emergency vehicle
11.	rkfertcui	The type of emergency vehicle needed in a Kachemak Bay town in the 1960s
12.	iodidtar	This is also called "The Last Great Race"

UNIT 7: SOME LOW POINTS

LESSON 33: CORDOVA BURNS

FACTS TO KNOW

Prince William Sound – Cordova, devastated by fire in May 1963, is located on this sound in the Gulf of Alaska on the east side of the Kenai Peninsula

Kennecott Copper Mines – At one time it was the largest copper mine in the world until it closed in 1938

COMPREHENSION QUESTIONS

1) What "almost fatal blow" did Cordova experience in 1938? What resource helped it bounce back? _____

_____

_____

_____

2) Where did the fire start? How did the firemen attempt to stop the spread of the fire?

_____

_____

_____

_____

_____

3) How much damage did the fire cause? _____

_____

_____

_____

_____

_____

4) How did many Cordovans react as the fire was spreading? How was their reaction different by 12:30p.m.? _____

_____

_____

_____

_____

_____

5) What were some of the groups that assisted Cordova after the fire? _____

_____

_____

_____

_____

_____

DISCUSSION QUESTION

(Discuss this question with your teacher or write your answer in essay form below. Use additional paper if necessary.)

What did Gov. William Egan say about Cordova when he came to survey the damage a few days after the fire?

_____

_____

_____

_____

_____

_____

_____

_____

_____

_____

_____

_____

_____

_____

_____

_____

ENRICHMENT ACTIVITY

Watch this short video to learn more about the salmon industry in Cordova:
https://www.youtube.com/watch?v=u_aIGVqKItw

LEARN MORE

Look for this book at your local library:
From Fish and Copper: Cordova's Heritage and Buildings. Nielsen, Nikki. Anchorage: Cordova Historical Society, 1984.

UNIT 7: SOME LOW POINTS

LESSON 34: FLOODWATERS FILL FAIRBANKS

FACTS TO KNOW

Chena River – Fairbanks river that flooded in August 1967

Fairbanks – Large city in the interior of Alaska that experienced massive flooding in the summer of 1967

Flood Control Act of 1968 – Largest federal civil works program in the state, created to prevent future flooding in the Fairbanks area

COMPREHENSION QUESTIONS

1) What were many Fairbanks residents doing as rain began to fall in July 1967? _____

_____

_____

_____

_____

_____

2) Describe what Sandy Vernon and her husband did when the floodwaters got to their house. _____

_____

_____

_____

_____

_____

3) What conditions made the rescue mission difficult? _____

_____

_____

_____

4) Where did many Fairbanks residents take shelter after the flood? _____

_____

_____

_____

_____

5) How much damage did the flood do? Were there any casualties? _____

_____

_____

_____

_____

DISCUSSION QUESTION

(Discuss this question with your teacher or write your answer in essay form below. Use additional paper if necessary.)

Do you remember other eyewitness accounts you read about in the chapter? Describe one of these accounts.

_____

_____

_____

_____

_____

_____

_____

_____

_____

_____

_____

_____

_____

_____

_____

_____

ENRICHMENT ACTIVITY

Compare and contrast the impact that the 1963 fire had on Cordova with the impact that the 1968 flood had on Fairbanks. How was it similar? How was it different? Write a short essay with supporting facts from Chapters 33 and 34.

LEARN MORE

Learn more about how floods form by visiting http://kids.nationalgeographic.com/explore/science/flood/#flood-house.jpg

UNIT 7: SOME LOW POINTS

LESSON 35: CONGRESSMEN DISAPPEAR

FACTS TO KNOW

Nicholas "Nick" Begich – Alaska congressman who disappeared along with U.S. House Majority Leader Hale Boggs, Begich aide Russell L. Brown and their pilot during a flight to Juneau in 1972

Don Jonz – Pilot who flew the plane that was lost in 1972 with U.S. Congressman Nick Begich on board

COMPREHENSION QUESTIONS

1) Why did Nick Begich and Hale Boggs decide to fly to Juneau in October 1972? ____

_____

_____

_____

_____

2) Describe the search effort for the Cessna 310. _____

_____

_____

_____

_____

_____

_____

3) How did this search make history? What made the search difficult? _____

_____

_____

_____

_____

_____

_____

4) When did the search officially end? What was the conclusion? _____

_____

_____

_____

_____

_____

5) What other mystery was discovered after the search? _____

_____
_____
_____
_____
_____

DISCUSSION QUESTION

(Discuss this question with your teacher or write your answer in essay form below. Use additional paper if necessary.)

What conspiracies emerged about the plane's disappearance?

_____
_____
_____
_____
_____
_____
_____
_____
_____
_____
_____
_____
_____
_____
_____
_____

TIME TO REVIEW

Review Chapters 29-35 of your book before moving on the Unit Review. See how many questions you can answer without looking at your book.

UNIT 6: SOME HIGHLIGHTS
UNIT 7: SOME LOW POINTS

REVIEW LESSONS 29-35

Write down what you remember about:

Cordova _____

_____

Iceworm _____

_____

Ohmer Waer _____

_____

Pachyderm _____

_____

Annabelle _____

_____

Alaska Zoo _____

_____

Homer _____

_____

General Mills _____

_____

Dorothy Page _____

_____

Joe Redington Sr. _____

_____

Iditarod Trail _____

_____

Dick Wilmarth _____

_____

Prince William Sound _____

_____

Kennecott Copper Mines _____

_____

Chena River _____

_____

Fairbanks _____

_____

Flood Control Act of 1968 _____

_____

Nicholas "Nick" Begich _____

_____

Don Jonz _____

_____

Fill in the blanks:

1) "Get me something that will make _____ and sell papers," the editor of the Klondike Nugget told newsman _____. As he pondered what sort of news might attract readers, a huge _____ hit the Canadian gold-rush town. That's when a great idea hit the newsman. He announced that new creatures had emerged after the storm: _____.

2) Residents of _____ rallied around an idea to make an _____ and have a celebration to shake off the winter blues.

3) Although many people believe _____ are fantasy, they do, indeed, exist and were first discovered in 1887 on Alaska's Muir _____. The tiny black _____ avoid the sun and spend their lives in _____.

4) Annabelle, born in _____ in 1964, was the first _____ in Alaska since the ice age. It all started when _____ saw an ad for a Chiffon toilet paper contest for grocers in 1966. The company announced: "$3,000 or _____" to the winner. The Anchorage grocer won the contest and startled the tissue paper executives when he said, "I'll take _____."

5) The _____, located on land adjacent to Sammye Seawell's ranch, opened in 1969 with _____ and other donated animals. The 30-acre park's name changed to _____ in June 1980 and served as a star attraction to draw thousands of visitors to see various Alaska animals. A female _____ named Maggie joined _____ as a companion in 1983.

6) Something magical happened at America's farthest-north zoo when trainers put a _____ into _____ trunk in 1991. She started _____ _____ in front of cheering visitors. Her _____ raised several hundred thousand dollars for the zoo.

7) Following the city of _____ incorporation in 1964, the city issued a monthly check to the _____ for operations, fuel and maintenance. But when the need for a new _____ arose in 1969, the city didn't have the money to buy one.

8) _____ residents turned to _____ after they learned about a promotion offered by _____. The nationally known company offered a program where people could turn in their _____ for large household items.

9) _____, secretary of the Aurora Dog Mushers Club, thought a _____ on the historic _____ – which originally began in _____ during the gold rush days and stretched to Knik, then through the gold camp of Iditarod and eventually to _____ – might revitalize a longtime Alaska tradition.

10) _____ talked to veteran musher _____ about her idea. His response, "_____!" has been echoed by hundreds of _____ from all parts of Alaska and the world ever since.

11) On March 3, _____, amid the cheers of hundreds of well-wishers, 34 _____ left _____ headed for _____ in pursuit of not only a dream, but also $50,000 in prize money pledged by _____. _____ crossed the finish line first and collected $12,000 in prize money.

12) The city of _____ took a hit in 1938 when the _____ closed down. The _____ was abandoned and the _____ sold for scrap. _____ had another resource to fall back on – _____ _____ provided employment for the people who stayed with the town.

13) Then, on May 2, _____, it faced one of its greatest challenges. _____'s residents awoke in the early hours to find a major _____ sweeping through their town. The _____ did not stop until 14 _____ had been destroyed and many more damaged, including City Hall and the fire department.

14) With the spirit and enthusiasm of pioneers past, _____'s citizens knuckled down and _____ their town. But this time they used different _____ – _____ buildings replaced wooden frames.

15) While many _____ residents were in the midst of the Alaska Purchase Centennial, celebrating the _____ purchase of Alaska from _____ in _____, water from the _____ River was steadily rising as 3.34 inches of rain fell on the city.

16) In order to escape the waist-high flood waters, _____ and her husband felt their way through water covering the _____ in pitch black conditions not knowing that the water was washing away the _____.

17) The flood put _____ and Nenana under as much as _____ of water. _____ people died, and damage was estimated at _____ million, according to the *Anchorage Daily News*.

18) The disappearance of Alaska's _____ on Oct. 16, 1972, sparked the most _____ for an aircraft in Alaska's history. _____ were in the sky within 90 minutes of the Federal Aviation Administration reporting the six-passenger aircraft had failed to land in _____.

19) The longest _____ in Alaska's history finally was called off on _____ as fresh snowfalls began covering the landscape. During its record-breaking _____, searchers traced down _____, flew more than _____ and covered more than _____ square miles at a cost of nearly _____.

20) Another _____ also surrounded this incident. Newspapers reported that pilot _____ employees had found the _____ that was thought to be in the missing _____ on their boss' desk at his Fairbanks office. They also found all the _____ known to them untouched in Fairbanks.

Some Low Points
Word Search
Please find the words in the list below

```
L  D  R  A  U  G  L  A  N  O  I  T  A  N  P  E  K  P  F  O
V  T  U  O  S  E  M  A  L  F  I  V  F  G  E  R  I  F  Q  Z
C  W  S  R  T  W  S  F  V  B  F  C  N  Q  N  W  V  C
C  I  V  I  L  A  I  R  P  A  T  R  O  L  U  E  R  M  O  L
E  Y  N  N  M  T  C  R  C  E  H  C  I  G  E  B  K  C  I  N
V  N  M  K  X  I  X  O  N  X  S  E  E  G  U  F  E  R  E  Y
R  E  K  R  E  X  E  K  L  O  Q  J  U  N  E  A  U  V  H  Y
E  M  P  V  A  X  T  R  N  Y  C  O  K  C  T  F  Z  O  P  Q
V  S  U  B  N  N  P  S  D  C  C  A  R  P  I  U  N  H  O  U
I  S  R  P  S  C  O  L  E  K  M  N  E  R  N  Q  H  D  R  Y
R  E  E  T  S  O  E  I  O  N  G  C  E  B  L  R  E  R  T  C
A  R  T  X  E  R  R  F  T  S  A  F  X  G  Y  D  V  R  S  F
N  G  A  V  C  D  L  Y  T  A  I  L  R  Z  R  T  A  F  A  A
E  N  W  R  I  O  E  B  N  G  V  O  P  L  H  E  B  P  T  I
H  O  Y  P  O  V  O  J  H  E  P  L  N  R  P  R  M  C  A  R
C  C  G  D  S  A  I  T  G  D  M  D  A  P  I  K  A  E  C  B
M  Y  D  C  T  L  E  E  C  C  E  X  A  S  E  A  T  J  R  A
S  M  U  S  M  R  E  F  M  D  I  S  A  S  T  E  R  A  C  N
G  N  L  Y  S  L  J  Z  N  P  I  P  I  D  W  A  T  Q  Q  K
D  B  S  N  O  E  E  M  U  D  J  E  H  C  R  A  E  S  W  S
```

CORDOVA
FLAMES
FLOOD
BOATS
SALVATION ARMY
NICK BEGICH
SEARCH
CONGRESSMEN
DISAPPEAR

FIRE
CATASTROPHE
FAIRBANKS
NATIONAL GUARD
REFUGEES
CESSNA
AIRPLANES
BEACON

EXPLOSION
FIREFIGHTERS
SLUDGY WATER
CHENA RIVER
DISASTER
JUNEAU
EMERGENCY LOCATOR
CIVIL AIR PATROL

UNIT 6: SOME HIGHLIGHTS
UNIT 7: SOME LOW POINTS

UNIT TEST

Choose *three* of the following questions to answer in paragraph form. Use as much detail as possible to completely answer the question. Use extra paper in back of the book if needed.

1) Which two people used the idea of an iceworm to create a buzz in Cordova? Summarize how they did this? What annual festival does Cordova celebrate surrounding the iceworm?

2) How did the first pachyderm in Alaska since the ice age come to Anchorage? What special talent did she have? What organization did she inspire in the 1960s?

3) How did the community of Homer receive a new firetruck for their town in the late 1960s? Include details about who was involved in the process and how it all came together. What did the fire chief at the time say about this story? What did it represent for their city?

4) What great race was born in the 1960s-1970s? Why was the race put on hold after its first race in 1967? Who won in 1973? Why did he have an advantage over many of his competitors?

5) Compare and contrast the impact that the 1963 fire had on Cordova with the impact that the 1968 flood had on Fairbanks. How was it similar? How was it different? Include details about each event in your answer.

6) How did the search for U.S. Congressman Nick Begich make history? What mysteries surrounded his disappearance? What conspiracies arose surrounding this event?

_____
_____
_____
_____
_____
_____
_____
_____
_____
_____
_____
_____

UNIT 6: SOME HIGHLIGHTS
UNIT 7: SOME LOW POINTS

    Review Questions   _____ (possible 19 pts.)

    Fill-the-Blanks   _____ (possible 20 pts.)

Unit Test

Essay 1

    Demonstrates understanding of the topic   _____ (possible 5 pts.)

    Answered the questions completely and accurately   _____ (possible 5 pts.)

    Composition is neat   _____ (possible 5 pts.)

    Grammar and Spelling   _____ (possible 5 pts.)

Essay 2

    Demonstrates understanding of the topic   _____ (possible 5 pts.)

    Answered the questions completely and accurately   _____ (possible 5 pts.)

    Composition is neat   _____ (possible 5 pts.)

    Grammar and Spelling   _____ (possible 5 pts.)

Essay 3

    Demonstrates understanding of the topic   _____ (possible 5 pts.)

    Answered the questions completely and accurately   _____ (possible 5 pts.)

    Composition is neat   _____ (possible 5 pts.)

    Grammar and Spelling   _____ (possible 5 pts.)

Subtotal Points _____ **(possible 99 pts.)**

Extra Credit

    Word Puzzle   _____ (5 pt. per completed puzzle)

    Complete an Enrichment Activity   _____ (possible 5 pts.)

    Oral presentation   _____ (possible 10 pts.)

    Total Extra Credit   _____

Total Unit Points _____

GRADE CHART

A   89-99+ points

B   79-88 points

C   69-78 points

D   59-68 points

NOTE TO TEACHERS/PARENTS

Chapters 36-39 in the section Mass Murder in the North, pages 359-400, contain details about historical murder cases that may be too graphic for some students/classroooms. Teachers can elect to assign these chapters for extra reading.

Please note: There are no workbook lessons 36-39 for these chapters.

Courtesy Alaska State Library

This photograph is from the Alaska Territorial Department of Education classroom at Gustavus in Southeast Alaska taken in 1931.

Gustavus, which was formerly known as Strawberry Point, is less than 100 years old. But Tlingits used the area for fishing, berry picking and other activities.

The first settlers arrived in 1914, but they did not stay. The first permanent homestead was established in 1917, when Abraham Lincoln Parker moved his family there.

Sources say many strawberries still may be found in the area.

UNIT 8: 25 YEARS IN THE NEWS

LESSON 40: 1960s IN THE NEWS

Summarize each event:

1) **1961: Survival story tops the news** _____

_____

_____

_____

_____

2) **1962: Japanese ship seized** _____

_____

_____

_____

_____

3) **1963: Crash victims survive more than a month in the wilderness** _____

_____

_____

_____

_____

4) **1966: St. Michael's Cathedral burns** _____

_____

_____

_____

_____

5) **1967: State motto** _____

_____

_____

_____

6) **1968: Sen. Ted Stevens** _____

_____

_____

_____

7) 1969: Alaskans receive first live feed from satellite _____

_____

_____

_____

_____

8) 1969: Gravel dreams up Dome City _____

_____

_____

_____

_____

DISCUSSION QUESTION

(Discuss this question with your teacher or write your answer in essay form below. Use additional paper if necessary.)

Which story from the 1960s was most interesting to you and why?

_____

_____

_____

_____

_____

_____

_____

_____

_____

_____

_____

_____

_____

ENRICHMENT ACTIVITY

Would you like to learn more about what happened in the news during the 1960s? See if you can find an interesting story about something that happened in Alaska during the 1960s by searching online or visiting the library. Write a short summary about the story and present it to your class.

LEARN MORE

See a beautiful satellite picture of Alaska by visiting http://www.livescience.com/37560-alaska-from-space.html

UNIT 8: 25 YEARS IN THE NEWS

LESSON 41: 1970s IN THE NEWS

Summarize each event:

1) **1971: Alaskans watch 1971 NFC championship game live** _____

_____
_____
_____
_____
_____

2) **1972: Benny Benson dies** _____

_____
_____
_____
_____
_____

3) **1974: Ernest Guening dies** _____

_____
_____
_____
_____

4) **1975: Wien Air Alaska crashes near Gambell** _____

_____
_____
_____
_____

5) **1976: Molly Hootch case** _____

_____
_____
_____
_____

6) 1978: D-2 Lands hot topic _____

_____

_____

_____

_____

7) 1979: Old Believers become U.S. citizens _____

_____

_____

_____

_____

8) 1979: Progress brings high prices _____

_____

_____

_____

_____

DISCUSSION QUESTION

(Discuss this question with your teacher or write your answer in essay form below. Use additional paper if necessary.)

Which story from the 1970s was more interesting to you and why?

_____

_____

_____

_____

_____

_____

ENRICHMENT ACTIVITY

Would you like to learn more about what happened in the news during the 1970s? See if you can find an interesting story about something that happened in Alaska during the 1970s by searching online or visiting the library. Write a short summary about the story and present it to your class.

LEARN MORE

Read about more news from the 1970s by visiting http://www.akhistorycourse.org/south-central-alaska/1970-1980-the-land-and-its-uses

UNIT 8: 25 YEARS IN THE NEWS

LESSON 42: 1980s IN THE NEWS

Summarize each event:

1) **1980: ANILCA passed** _____

_____

_____

_____

_____

2) **1982: First PFD checks issues** _____

_____

_____

_____

_____

_____

3) **1983: Time zones changed** _____

_____

_____

_____

_____

_____

4) **1984: Respected Native leader dies** _____

_____

_____

_____

_____

_____

5) **1984: Alaska celebrates 25 years of statehood** _____

_____

_____

_____

_____

_____

6) 1984: Russians seize Homer ship _____

_____
_____
_____
_____

DISCUSSION QUESTION

(Discuss this question with your teacher or write your answer in essay form below. Use additional paper if necessary.)

Which story from the 1980s was most interesting to you and why?

_____
_____
_____
_____
_____
_____
_____
_____
_____
_____
_____
_____
_____
_____

TIME TO REVIEW

Review Chapters 40-42 of your book before moving on the Unit Review. See how many questions you can answer without looking at your book.

Alaskans celebrated the Last Frontier's 25th anniversary as a state throughout 1984. Picnics, ceremonies and festivities were planned and many communities, like Juneau seen in this photograph, filled the northern skies with fireworks.

UNIT 8: 25 YEARS IN THE NEWS

REVIEW LESSONS 40-42

Fill in the blanks:

1) **1961: Survival story tops news**
The survival story of _____ William C. Waters, a _____
tourist lost for 69 days in the subarctic wilderness northeast of _____, was
the No. 1 story for 1961. When two _____ finally found him sitting along a
creek many miles north on Aug. 27, about 100 pounds lighter and nearly _____,
Waters became the subject of widespread national and international publicity.

2) **1967: State Motto**
The state motto, "_____," became official on Oct. 1, 1967, by an
act passed by the Alaska Legislature, which also directed that the motto be put on

_____.

3) **1968: Sen. Ted Stevens**
Alaska Gov. _____ appointed Anchorage attorney
Ted Stevens to the U.S. Senate on Dec. 24, 1968, to fill the seat left vacant when
_____ died in office on Dec. 11.

4) **1969: Alaskans receive first live feed from satellite**
Alaskans had a front-row seat to watch astronaut _____ plant the first
footsteps on the moon on _____, when the first live satellite tele-
cast came to _____. Legendary Alaska broadcast pioneer August G.
"Augie" Hiebert birthed television in Alaska with KTVA. Following that historic step,
Alaska leapt forward with satellites providing _____
and other high-speed communications of the day.

5) **1974: Ernest Gruening dies**
After a long and illustrious career serving Alaska as a politician and statesman,
Ernest Gruening died on June 26, 1974, at the age of 87. He served as Alaska's
_____, an activist for _____ and U.S. senator.
Gruening also was one of the first to fight for the rights and wellbeing of Alaska's
_____. His ashes were scattered on a mountaintop above Juneau.

6) 1976: Molly Hootch case

The suit of Tobeluk v. Lind, known by most as the Molly Hootch case, was settled in 1976. A detailed decree provided for the establishment of a _____ program in all 126 _____ covered by the litigation, unless people in the _____ decided against a local program. Prior to this, children who wanted to go to _____ had no choice but to leave their _____.

7) 1980: ANILCA passed

Congress passed the _____ on Nov. 12, 1980, and President _____ signed it into law on Dec. 2 that year. The act provided varying degrees of special protection to more than 150 million acres of land in Alaska, doubling the size of the country's _____ and tripling the amount of land designated as _____. It was called the most significant _____ measure in the history of the nation.

8) 1983: Time zones changed

Time zones shifted to include all Alaska, except _____, to one zone called _____ in 1983. It made most Alaska time one hour _____ than Pacific Standard Time, which helped businesses and the military communicate most of the day within and outside of the state.

9) 1984: Alaska celebrates 25 years of statehood

Alaskans celebrated the state's 25th anniversary throughout 1984, including at a _____ in the Wood Center at the _____ that January. A wall-size reproduction of the _____ that commemorated the special year was at the head of the table.

UNIT 8: 25 YEARS IN THE NEWS

UNIT TEST

Answer *all* of the following questions in paragraph form. Use as much detail as possible to completely answer the question. Use extra paper in back of the book if needed.

1) Name at least three major news stories in Alaska from the 1960s. Why were each of these events important?

2) Name at least three major news stories in Alaska from the 1970s. Why were each of these events important?

3) Name at least three major news stories in Alaska from the 1980s. Why were each of these events important?

_____
_____
_____
_____
_____
_____
_____
_____
_____
_____
_____
_____
_____
_____
_____
_____
_____
_____
_____
_____
_____
_____

UNIT 8: 25 YEARS IN THE NEWS

Fill-the-Blanks _____ (possible 9 pts.)

Unit Test

Essay 1
Demonstrates understanding of the topic _____ (possible 5 pts.)
Answered the questions completely and accurately _____ (possible 5 pts.)
Composition is neat _____ (possible 5 pts.)
Grammar and Spelling _____ (possible 5 pts.)

Essay 2
Demonstrates understanding of the topic _____ (possible 5 pts.)
Answered the questions completely and accurately _____ (possible 5 pts.)
Composition is neat _____ (possible 5 pts.)
Grammar and Spelling _____ (possible 5 pts.)

Essay 3
Demonstrates understanding of the topic _____ (possible 5 pts.)
Answered the questions completely and accurately _____ (possible 5 pts.)
Composition is neat _____ (possible 5 pts.)
Grammar and Spelling _____ (possible 5 pts.)

Subtotal Points _____ **(possible 69 pts.)**

Extra Credit
Word Puzzle _____ (5 pt. per completed puzzle)
Complete an Enrichment Activity _____ (possible 5 pts.)
Oral presentation _____ (possible 10 pts.)

Total Extra Credit _____

Total Unit Points _____

GRADE CHART

A   62-69+ points

B   55-61 points

C   48-54 points

D   41-47 points

EXTRA PAPER FOR LESSONS

EXTRA PAPER FOR LESSONS

EXTRA PAPER FOR LESSONS

EXTRA PAPER FOR LESSONS

EXTRA PAPER FOR LESSONS

EXTRA PAPER FOR LESSONS

EXTRA PAPER FOR LESSONS